In *Reclaimed Textiles*, leading textile artist Kim Thittichai demonstrates how to repurpose discarded materials and packaging to create new, stunning artworks. From making evening dresses out of plastic carrier bags to weaving boxes from cardboard packaging, or making textile art from vintage lace and photographs, this book inspires and encourages you to see a new life in everything around you.

This book is a celebration of the handmade – from patchwork, rag-rugging, stitching and weaving, to quilting, collage and appliqué.

By becoming more resourceful in your work, you can create works that are cost-effective, greener and full of history. As well as an introduction to the basic techniques, tools and materials that you might use in your textile work, there are chapters on textiles, paper, packaging, plastic and mixed media, each showcasing the work of the best students and artists working in textiles today.

Reclaimed Textiles

Reclaimed Textiles

TECHNIQUES FOR PAPER, STITCH, PLASTIC AND MIXED MEDIA

Kim Thittichai

BATSFORD

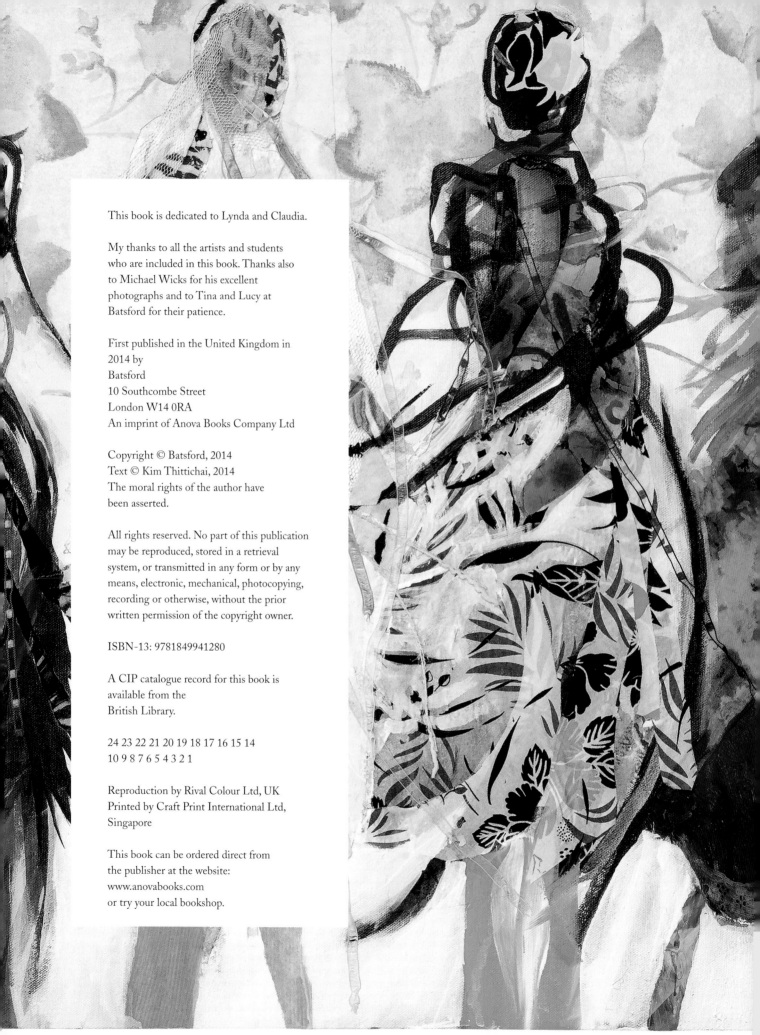

This book is dedicated to Lynda and Claudia.

My thanks to all the artists and students who are included in this book. Thanks also to Michael Wicks for his excellent photographs and to Tina and Lucy at Batsford for their patience.

First published in the United Kingdom in 2014 by
Batsford
10 Southcombe Street
London W14 0RA
An imprint of Anova Books Company Ltd

ISBN-13: 9781849941280

A CIP catalogue record for this book is available from the British Library.

24 23 22 21 20 19 18 17 16 15 14
10 9 8 7 6 5 4 3 2 1

Reproduction by Rival Colour Ltd, UK
Printed by Craft Print International Ltd, Singapore

This book can be ordered direct from the publisher at the website:
www.anovabooks.com
or try your local bookshop.

Contents

Introduction   6

Basic techniques   8

Inspiration   14

Working with textiles   18

Working with paper   42

Working with packaging   62

Working with plastics   76

Working with mixed media   96

Conclusion   118

Featured artists   120

Useful addresses and suppliers   122

Bits and blogs   123

Further reading   124

Index   126

Glossary   127

Introduction

ABOVE My family with homemade Gooby Dolls.

Most of the crafts we enjoy today were once thrift crafts. Patchwork, rag-rugging and appliqué were all skills that reused textiles to create items to make the home more comfortable; weaving, too, came in useful for turning strips of worn fabric into rugs. Our country has a long and fascinating history of 'make do and mend', particularly during (and after) the war years. It is only in my lifetime that clothes, furniture and all the 'things' we love to buy to decorate ourselves and our homes have become so readily available. Factories churn out the same product in many colourways, from shirts to cars, and we have never been so bombarded with merchandise. But, as in all things, we are going full circle – back to thinking about where things come from, and just in the nick of time, before the skills disappear, there is a groundswell of interest in the old,

traditional skills. These skills emphasize and celebrate the handmade as opposed to the mass-made.

Imagine never buying any materials or products for your craft again – could you do it? We are all such textile junkies these days, magpies flitting to the latest gorgeous things that are available to buy. The techniques and skills for these crafts are still the same, but we are just using more expensive (and perhaps easier to find) components to work with. It is all too easy to click your mouse and buy via the Internet. How many of you have a least one drawer of products you have stored away and never used? Do you even know why you bought them? I think that many of us are now feeling the guilt of storing away things we are never going to use. Judging by the amount of job lots that are now available on a certain auction website, I think more and more of us are starting to think about clearing out and cleaning up our act – if only for the space we would gain! And more space to create must be a better thing.

Many of us were brought up wearing handmade clothes. My mother always made my school summer dresses and knitted my jumpers and cardigans. I can remember a particularly vibrant orange nylon cable cardigan with a matching hat. She also made some of our toys from old clothes. My sister and I had a fabulous box of old clothes bought from jumble sales as

our dressing-up box. My sister wore my hand-me-down clothes and only occasionally had anything new. This type of recycling was the norm in the 1950s, 1960s and 1970s.

Is it really necessary to buy beautifully colour-coordinated packs of fabric that are cut to size for patchwork projects, from bags to full-sized bed quilts? There is nothing wrong with creating patchwork from old clothes found at a car-boot sale. The drawbacks to pre-cut fabric are that you don't have to think about the colours you are working with because someone else has done that for you, and there is every chance your work will look very similar to the next person's. Is that what you want? Being different can be a little unnerving, but give it try: you might like it! I appreciate that colour can be tricky to work with. You may already have several books on your bookshelf that will give you some idea of how to start choosing the colours you want to work with. If not, there are many tutors who run workshops on colour and the use of it, who would love to help.

Unusual and more difficult to find materials and media will make your work much more individual and far more interesting. Is this food for thought? An infinite number of textures and colours are out there: you just have to want to find them. Many of them will be in your house right now; you just haven't noticed they are there. I am not trying to start a revolt – I am just asking you to think about what you are using in your work and how you acquire it. We can all at least try to include some reused items on our work and this will create interesting challenges. Personal objects, too, can add meaning to a piece of work, and viewers may recognize objects that are part of their own shared experience and social history.

This book is by no means meant to be thorough study of what is happening in the recycled textiles world of today. It is more of a gentle ramble in and around some of the areas I have discovered that have inspired and interested me in my time as a travelling textiles tutor – or just made me laugh. It covers work created by students of all ages, from those who are not particularly able to artists who earn a living from their art. The sourcing of work for this book has been similar to curating an exhibition. My choice of the different artists' work is designed to inspire you and illustrate certain points, and I hope you enjoy it. The contact details of all the artists are at the back of the book, along with links to websites you may find interesting.

BELOW Newspaper decorated with foiled Hot Spots and herringbone stitch.

Basic techniques

Free machining into printed Solufleece

1 Solufleece is a water-soluble machine-embroidery product that will take heavy needling. As it is water-soluble you would think it would dissolve if you printed onto it with wet paint – but not if you stretch it first. Choose your printing block: it can be a commercial one, one you have made yourself, or even a potato cut in half.

2 Stretch the Solufleece in an embroidery frame, making it sure it is tight. When you pull the fabric to tighten it, take care not to rip it. Print onto the stretched Solufleece with your printing block using a sponge to apply the paint. Take care not to add too much paint – you just need enough to leave a complete print. If you apply too much paint the Solufleece will dissolve. Test how much paint, you need on a spare piece of paper. Wait for it to dry.

ABOVE A wooden printing block.
BELOW The printed Solufleece stretched in a frame.

ABOVE Stitching onto the print.
BELOW A completed, stitched print.

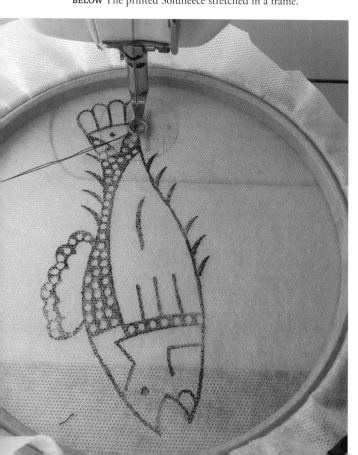

ABOVE Detail of *Little Fishes*, see page 112.

3 Set up your sewing machine for free machine embroidery. Drop the feed dogs and attach a darning foot. Using the print as your guide, free machine all over the print with several layers of stitch, making sure all the stitches link up. (If the stitches don't link up, you work will fall apart when you dissolve the Solufleece in water.)

4 Dissolve the Solufleece carefully in warm water. If you can gently stretch your stitched print on a board and anchor it with pins it will help keep your stitches in shape. When the Solufleece is completely dissolved, pat the now freestanding stitches with kitchen towel to remove most of the water and lay out flat and leave to dry out.

5 Your stitched shape can now be applied to any project. It can be stuck onto a canvas that needs a bit of 'lift' or can be hand stitched into place. This technique was used for the lacy fish shown above and the fern in the piece on page 55.

Painted Bondaweb

You will need:
• Bondaweb
• Water-based paints
• A background fabric
• Baking parchment
• Jones Tones heat transfer foils
• Dot Jewels, mica flakes, gilding flakes, dried pressed flowers or seeds
• Iron

Bondaweb is the most versatile product I have ever worked with. It can be used in dressmaking, quilting and virtually every craft in one way or another. Bondaweb is a fine layer of heat-transferable glue on a backing carrier paper. It can even be ironed onto wood – see page 111.

When painting Bondaweb, do so with a thin layer of water-based paint. The paint needs to be thin, otherwise the Bondaweb will not stick to whatever you are ironing it onto. As a guide, water down acrylics by half. Using water-based paints as opposed to oil-based ones will cut out any fumes that may occur when oil-based colouring media is heated.

ABOVE Dot jewels and mica flakes.

ABOVE Painted Bondaweb.

Instructions

1 Prepare your work surface with layers of newspaper. Taking a 5cm (2in) decorators' paint brush, gently apply water to the rough (glue) side of the Bondaweb. After a minute you will see the Bondaweb ripple. Once this happens, apply the watered down paint, again to the rough side of the Bondaweb. Paint in the direction of the ripples – this helps to avoid a subtle crosshatched effect which can be distracting when the Bondaweb is ironed off. Leave to dry overnight. The Bondaweb must be completely dry before you use it.

2 Cut your dry painted Bondaweb to the size you need and iron onto your chosen surface rough/glue side down. Important – *always* use baking parchment underneath and on top of your work; Bondaweb will stick to your iron. Use a hot iron.

ABOVE Colourful Thoughts multi-surface paints, ideal for painting Bondaweb.

ABOVE Painted Bondaweb cut to shape and ironed onto black cotton using baking parchment to protect the iron.

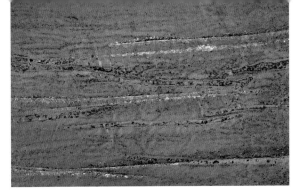

ABOVE Painted Bondaweb decorated with slashes of heat transfer foil.

ABOVE Then decorated with mica flakes...

ABOVE Then with Dot Jewels...

3 Wait for the Bondaweb to cool and then remove the baking parchment and the backing paper.

4 You now have an exposed area of coloured glue to play with. The embellishments in this section are just suggestions. Many fibres and glittery media can be applied to Bondaweb, from wool and silk tops to glitter and sequins.

5 To decorate your painted Bondaweb with slashes of heat-transfer foil, lay your foil colour-side up onto top of your painted Bondaweb. Cover with a sheet of baking parchment and, using the side of the iron with it facing away from your body, run the iron over the baking parchment slowly. There is no need to press hard; it is the heat that does the work. Remove the baking parchment and the foil. Wherever you have applied the heat, the foil should have stuck to the painted Bondaweb.

6 You can also add all manner of glittery media – here I have used mica flakes. Mica is a mineral and has a lustre rather than the flash of glitter. Just sprinkle a thin layer over exposed painted Bondaweb and iron in place, making sure you continue to use baking parchment to cover your work when you iron the media in place.

7 Dot Jewels have been added to this sample but you could use sequins instead.

8 I usually decorate my painted Bondaweb samples with hand stitch, but this surface will also look fabulous machine stitched into. When working with a new process, it is great fun to see how far you can go and just how much will stick. Just bear in mind that Bondaweb can look beautiful undecorated – you don't need to add too many embellishments.

BELOW Painted and decorated Bondaweb finished with hand stitch.

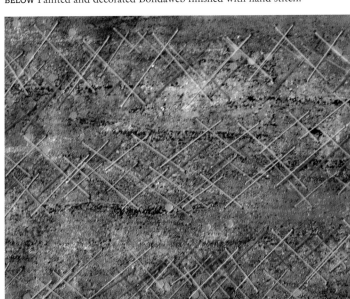

Heat distressing foil food packaging

Food packaging comes in many different colours printed into a matt or foil surface. The foil surfaces are great fun to texture with heat. Warning – whenever heating food packaging, always work in a well-ventilated room. While it is unlikely that food packaging will give off fumes (it is created to wrap food, after all) I can't guarantee it won't. Packaging and what it is made from is changing all the time.

The way to test if your packaging is suitable to distress with heat is to squeeze it into a ball in your hand, if the packaging goes back to its usual shape, that will distress. If the ball stays in shape, as with tin/aluminium foil then this won't work.

Choose your food packaging; in this case I have used chocolate wrappers. Lay the wrappers between baking parchment and lightly iron at a medium setting, keeping the iron moving slowly. When I am teaching this process I call it the 'Kiss, Stroke and Caress' ironing technique. I know it sounds a bit silly, but if you use humorous terms they are easier to recall.

You will see the wrappers moving; stop when you think you have enough texture – it will only take a few seconds. You are left with a colourful, shiny surface which is soft enough to stitch into by hand or machine.

For examples, see the flower brooches on page 72.

ABOVE Foil wrappers are ideal for heat distressing.

Melting plastic products

Since writing the chapter on plastics in my first book, *Hot Textiles*, plastics, and how we make, use and dispose of them, have changed. While they are still made from roughly the same materials, great care needs to be taken when melting them. Always work in a well-ventilated room and if you can smell the plastic – stop! Printed plastic may look exciting but the print may give off fumes. Working with this in small quantities it is very unlikely to harm you, however, I would stress that anyone who has breathing problems or is pregnant takes extra care and wears a respirator mask. Never take chances. One extra word of warning: molten plastic is hot and will stick to your skin and burn you, so please do be careful.

For examples of the use of melted plastic, see chapter 4.

BELOW Chocolate-bar wrappers ironed lightly between baking parchment to create a 'bubbled' texture.

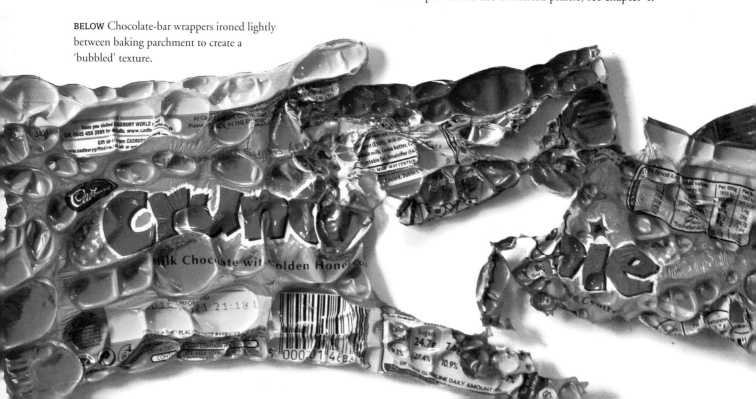

Sort out your collection of plastic bags and plastic food packaging and decide which ones you are gong to use. You won't need more than one or two bags. Lay the packaging onto baking parchment and cover the plastic with a sheet of baking parchment. With gentle pressure and a hot iron, iron the whole surface slowly. The plastics will fuse together. The longer you leave the iron on the plastic, the thinner and more lacy it will become. Depending on the thickness of the finished fused piece it can be hand stitched or machine stitched into.

Mixed-media 'wet' products

There can be great confusion when trying to identify the wet media that an artist has used when creating their mixed-media work. There is a comprehensive glossary at the back of this book listing most of the products used throughout.

In my work I use and can recommend the following:

Gel medium An acrylic paste that can be used both as a glue and as a varnish. It has a milky appearance and dries clear and water resistant. If you buy the thicker version this can be watered down to paint onto your work.

Acrylic wax This is another acrylic product and will dry clear and water-resistant to give a soft, lustre finish. I use it to seal most of my work.

RIGHT Texture gels and Xpandaprint (front), foil glue and acrylic wax (back).

Foil glue
A glue that never quite 'dries'. It stays sticky to the touch. Foil glue comes in pens or squeezy bottles. When it has gone clear you can press transfer foil onto it (colour-side up). This is great for 3D projects where you need to use foil but can't use an iron and Bondaweb. Foil glue can be piped, printed and applied with a palette knife to great effect.

Xpandaprint This a creamy paste that can printed with, squidged through a stencil or simply painted on in a thin layer. It is important to use this product sparingly – if you apply it too thickly the product will puff up into large balls that will just roll off your work. Once applied the Xpandaprint is heated and expanded with a heat gun to give a textured effect. Xpandaprint can be applied to any surface that will take heat.

ABOVE Plastic food packaging, ideal for experimenting with heat treatment.

ABOVE Now the food packaging that has been melted between baking parchment.

Inspiration

rehabilitate · reinstate · rescue · recover · repossess · retrieve · refit · rebuild · reform · reconstitute · reconstruct · regenerate · remodel · renovate · repair · revolutionize · restore · revamp · reawaken · reinvigorate · rejuvenate · revive · renewal · reprocess · reuse · rebirth · re-create · reorganize · reassemble · recondition · repossess · revivify · rehash · rework · rejoin · reincarnation · revitalize · refresh · reanimate · resurrect · reawaken · restore · recall · replenish · rehabilitate · refurbish · reintroduce · reveal · rethink · reassess · reconsider · re-evaluate · re-examine · remember · reflect · revise · re-source · repurpose

We must all now be familiar with 'upcycling' and 'vintage'; they are fast becoming the norm. 'Upcycling' is the process of converting waste materials or useless products into new materials or products of better quality or for better environmental value. 'Vintage' is a generic term for clothing or items originating from a previous era, whether new or second-hand. Open any of the popular craft magazines and you will find projects that re-create, for example turning a shabby coat into a bag or an old jumper into a hat.

There are so many choices and ways to buy clothes, groceries, and even the homes we now live in. It takes time, thought and effort to sort out our recycling every week. Many of us are doing our very best to 'save the earth' – a slogan that was very common a few years ago. We have come a long way since then, with roadside recycling collections outside our homes, and recycling bins for every kind of product and material outside superstores and the amenity tip. You may even have access to a local 'scrap store'.

Scrap stores take reusable, safe, clean waste products (scrap) and redistribute them. Usually these materials come from local industries and are donated, although there is a cost to the scrap store in terms of collection and sorting etc. The benefit to businesses is that they are able to get rid of material that they would normally pay to dispose of and that they are seen to play a part in their local community. Scrap stores are significantly different from scrapyards that deal in metal; the reuse element tends to be dominated by art and craft activities, and they are often aimed at those working with young children and schools and colleges. Most scrap stores operate with a small annual or monthly fee.

Many towns and cities all over the world hold markets of second-hand goods, which often include

haberdashery. Looking through other people's discarded threads and sewing equipment can be a great delight. Old threads, in particular, have become quite precious. Often dyed many years ago, in dye lots no longer used, they can prove to be a source of unusual colours. The choice of thread can make or break a piece of work, so it is always a good idea to collect threads wherever you can find them. You can build a reasonably inexpensive collection of threads in this way, from everyday machine sewing threads to precious jewel-coloured silks.

While it is very important and very worthy to recycle, it is also a great opportunity to have fun! Think, as you are sorting your rubbish – how could I use this? Can I use this? Be more selective when you buy food. Do you prefer chocolate in a purple wrapper or a bright pink one? Decisions, decisions. If you have old fabrics or garments that you think you can't use, unpick them, paint them, fray them, print on them, dye them, pleat them, tear them, stitch them – or all of the above. I think we are becoming less afraid of making a mess and experimenting now. If you look at social networking websites and the Internet, you will find artists from all over the world who are making a living from recycling all manner of things, from car tyres to bottle tops. I have a sculpture in my garden made from car hubcaps!

Working with fabrics that have a history can be far more satisfying than buying a metre of fabric off a roll. Admittedly, the fabric may be coming from a dress that you need to unpick before you can start your project, and these things take time, but slowing down can be a good thing. You have time to arrange your thoughts and new ideas have time to float into your mind. Most of us are so busy, rushing here and there. We need to slow down. It is a win-win situation.

BELOW Fish sculpture made from hubcaps by Ptolemy Elrington.

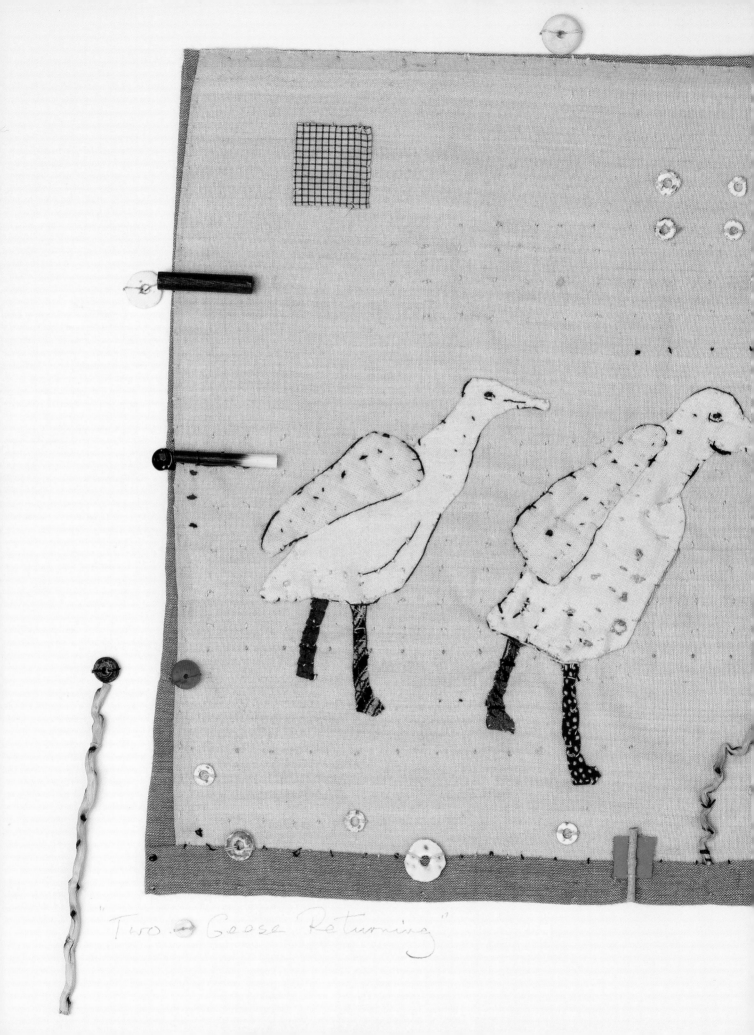

"Two Geese Returning"

Janet Bolton

Janet Bolton

An example of someone who has taken reuse to heart and created new and inspiring art pieces from the lost and found is textile artist Janet Bolton. Janet was one of my first 'inspirations' when I started teaching my course, Experimental Textiles, in 2000. Her delicate and well-considered use of the most homely and distressed fabrics made me realize that we don't all need perfect fabrics to work with. The fact that Janet used very little fabric in her work and only the simplest hand-sewing techniques also fascinated me. She was able to portray her subject without layering lots of different textures and colours – truly, less was more!

Janet has been exhibiting and teaching internationally since 1992, when she first exhibited at the Crafts Council in London. Her work is in many private collections, including the British Council's collection, the Crafts Council's permanent collection and the Embroiderers' Guild museum collection.

Two Geese Returning is constructed of two layers of fabric hand stitched together. One of the things I like best about Janet's work is that you can see her more functional stitches as well the more decorative ones that always embellish her work. Her use of unusual additions in her wall hangings is always intriguing. On the middle left of this work you can see half of a spent matchstick that has been couched on.

LEFT *Two Geese Returning*
by Janet Bolton.

Working with Textiles

Working with textiles

It has never been so easy to access recycled materials. We can wander around car-boot sales, visit charity shops and even have the hassle of sorting through old clothes removed by visiting vintage shops. Few of us actually need to work with recycled components; we are not living through the war years. It is, however, a choice many are making and it is fascinating to see what can be done with an old sock, jumper, or even a textile project that hasn't worked out.

Working with discarded and unwanted fabrics and garments can be a challenge. Knitted fabrics can run and ladder; unpicking garments can leave needle marks where seams once were – but surely that is part of the charm? The actual process of dismantling a garment may lead you to think more about the potential of the fabric you have in your hands. As you handle the fabric, ask yourself questions: Will it drape? Is it too stiff for my project? Is the fabric a little too thin for what I had in mind? Can I iron on an interfacing to help with this? Hopefully, new ideas will come to you as you work.

Jan Messent

Using the old, the discarded or the unwanted in your work will not in any way prevent you from creating beautiful results. Take the work of Jan Messent, for example. Jan qualified as a teacher in the mid-1950s but always wanted to embroider. When she retired from teaching, she became deeply involved with embroidery as an art form. She has written twenty-five books on embroidery, design, crochet and knitting – an amazing resource – and is a talented writer, artist and historian. She manages to make the combination of ancient embroideries and historical facts fascinating, and at times very amusing. I first became aware of her when I started teaching, and I continue to refer to her books. Her most recent books are *Celtic, Viking and Anglo-Saxon Embroidery* and *Embroidered Portraits: Ideas, Inspiration and Techniques*. Jan has lectured and delivered workshops internationally and is a keen member of the Embroiderers' Guild.

As with many textile artists, Jan is now looking at old work in a new light. Can it be reused? If a project hasn't worked out quite as you thought it would, do you have the courage to cut it up and transform it? Fabric and paper are very resilient: they can be stitched, unpicked, cut, torn, frayed or repainted.

In the image, the embroidered text reads:

IN·BASINGESTOCH HUNDRED·THE·KING·HOLDS· BASINGSTOCHES·IN·LORD SHIP·IT·HAS·ALWAYS·BEEN A·ROYAL·MANOR

LAND·FOR·20·PLOUGHS IN·LORDSHIP·12·PLOUGHS 20·VILLAGERS 8·SMALLHOLDERS 6·SLAVES

3·MILLS 12·FREEDMEN A·MARKET 20·ACRES·of·MEADOW WOODS·FOR·20·PIGS

THE·CHURCH OF·MONT·ST·MICH HOLDS·I·CHURCH THE·KING·IN·T MANOR·of·BASINGES

The Basingstoke Domesday Book

How many of us are happy to cut up a piece of work that hasn't worked out?

Measuring approximately 115 x 15cm (45 x 6in), this beautiful, concertina-shaped book has been made by recycling other work. It contains excerpts of the entry for Basingstoke in the Domesday Book and was made for an exhibition featuring Basingstoke.

Jan's book is constructed from an embroidered panel featuring architectural forms. Once the 'pages' of the book had been cut out, they were 'distressed' by spraying with walnut ink and adding daubs of paint and other media, to make them look well used. The cover of the book is a patchwork of leftovers from other pieces of work. The words inside have been embroidered over older embroideries.

LEFT This colourful and sturdy little book by Jan Messant is an excellent example of how you can create something beautiful from pieces of work that haven't turned out as initially planned.

Sarah Patterson

Jan Messent's work shows what an experienced textile artist can achieve, but what about the less experienced? Sarah Patterson is an art teacher at Portsmouth College, whose inspired teaching encompasses modern methods such as the use of computers and reuse of materials to unleash her students' creative flair. Sarah is always looking out for new processes and techniques within textiles to teach her students, but also uses more traditional methods such as batik and silk painting. When not teaching, Sarah is a keen crafter, specializing in personalized, unique gifts and soft furnishings for the home.

I first 'met' Sarah when she sent me some images of her students' work. As my first book, *Hot Textiles*, had been part of the inspiration for their work, Sarah thought I might be interested: I was very interested. The body of work consisted of several dresses created from black bin liners on the theme of the Little Black Dress. The collection of dresses was featured in several national shows and is still one of the most popular posts on my blog (see page 123). After seeing a brilliant exhibition of work by Sarah's students at a Creative Stitches show, including this tie dress, I asked if the dress shown left could be included in this book.

Anna Lee Wood: the tie dress

The tie dress is an exam piece constructed by AS/A2 Textile student Anna Lee Wood. The theme of the exam was 'Combinations and Alliances', and the brief was to deconstruct and reconstruct recycled textiles to give them new life, using combinations of material to create interesting garments. Anna chose to use ties sourced from charity shops.

She started her project by researching designers such as Gary Harvey, who has created 'eco-couture' collections inspired by vintage couture and made entirely from recycled clothing. The collections aimed to raise awareness of limited natural resources and the environmental issues involved in sending unwanted clothing to landfill, and to generate respect for the craftsmanship in recycling/upcycling.

Anna produced various experiments using the ties, which fed into the final piece. The ties were unpicked and deconstructed to be remade into this stunning dress. Anna has gone on to do a BA in Graphics at Portsmouth University.

RIGHT *Fabulous Landscape* by Angie Hughes (see page 24). This is a working sample to help develop ideas for a workshop. Created from strips of sari silk and machine stitch on a medium-weight interfacing.

Angie Hughes

Angie Hughes is a textile artist and tutor based in Ledbury, Herefordshire. She has been interested in textiles since she left school, although only discovered creative embroidery in 1994 when she began studying for a City and Guilds qualification at Malvern Hills College. While a student, she won the prestigious Charles Henry Foyle Trust Award for Stitched Textiles with her piece Unfolding Word, and had Shroud accepted for 'Art of the Stitch', an international biennial textile exhibition.

Angie's artwork is inspired by many themes, but particularly poetry or text and the natural world. She is well known for her glittering workshops, use of plant imagery and layers of velvet and stitch. Angie has taught internationally as well as for guilds and groups all over the UK. She has written a book, *Stitch, Cloth Paper & Paint*, on mixed-media textiles, and her work has featured in many publications.

Angie is a member of the Textile Study Group, a group of nationally and internationally recognized textile artists and tutors well known for innovative and challenging approaches to art practice and contemporary teaching.

Fabulous Landscape

Below is one of Angie's samples, made to test out ideas for a new workshop on creating landscapes from shredded sari silk, which is sold in balls that are ready to knit or stitch with. She laid the strips of sari silk on light iron-on interfacing to hold them together and help reinforce the work, then embellished them with embroidery. In the workshop, students are encouraged to try both free machine embroidery and set stitches. It is a great way to learn new stitches and revisit old ones. Hand stitch can be used in place of, or as well as, machine stitch.

RIGHT AND PREVIOUS PAGE
Fabulous Landscape by Angie Hughes was made for a workshop developed to encourage students to learn new, set machine stitches and maybe try their hand at free machine embroidery. Tonal value can be created by using darker and lighter strips of fabric.

Kim Thittichai

'I am having a clear-out – would you like any fabric?' How often do we hear those words and think that we daren't accumulate any more fabrics, as we have so many already. However, I knew that my friend Eleanor had some wonderful old sari fabrics and vintage lamé. Eleanor was a great collector of anything that sparkled: a lady after my own heart.

Vintage lamé sample

Lamé cloth is woven from a combination of metallic yarns and synthetic fibres such as nylon. The fabric has a shimmering, iridescent surface that catches and reflects light and shows movement in a striking way.

ABOVE Lamé fabrics ironed onto a light iron-on interfacing and then hand stitched with herringbone stitch in toning embroidery threads. Using toning thread will help the stitches blend into the work but still add texture.

Because the cloth is metallic, it can fray very easily and so needs some kind of fine, iron-on support to help when stitching into it. Eleanor's lamé fabrics were made in the same pattern or weave but in different colourways. I should imagine that she couldn't decide between the colours and so chose all of them. I machine-stitched different coloured strips of lamé together. I then ironed the sample on to a light iron-on interfacing to stop it slipping around and to reinforce it. Next, I applied machine stitching and hand stitching to decorate the seams. The finished sample would make quite a robust covering for a book, or it could be made into a bag by lining it and adding a handle.

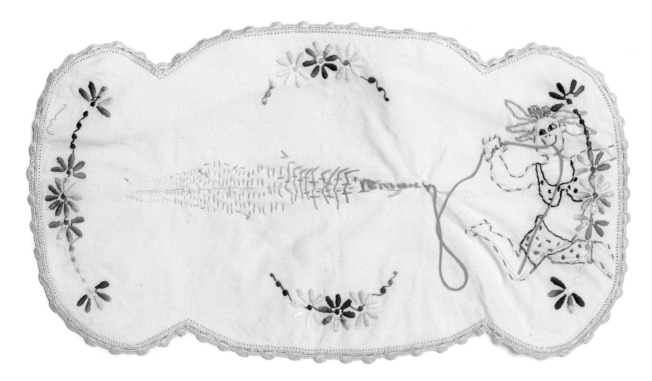

Val Griffiths-Jones

British-born Val Griffiths-Jones has always been creative. At a young age, she was taught 'the correct way' to do blanket stitch, and to make perfect buttonholes and the neatest of continuous strip openings. She became a medical photographer, but her life changed when she married and went to live in New Zealand in 1971.

Her creative side began to find a theme when she enrolled in a fabric art class and was encouraged to use the domestic fabric techniques in which she was already skilled to explore the themes of her immediate experience. The Fabric Art Company, a group of eight women who met each other for the first time at the class, emerged. This chance meeting proved to be magical: to quote a local newspaper, 'Out of the ashes of suburban domesticity has flared an artistic cooperative that has set Wellington alight with its wit, imagination and talent'. Val worked with the Fabric Art Company to produce the 'Stuffed Stuff Show', a witty, collaborative project of soft sculpture that brought crowds to thirteen

ABOVE AND LEFT *Woman Tired of Mending – Ran Away.*
RIGHT *I Made My Bed – I Lay On It.* A linen tray cloth hand stitched to depict a wedding secene taken from a photograph.

galleries throughout New Zealand. Her subsequent solo show, 'Stuffing On', consisted of twenty-five soft sculpture works. The pieces took about four years to make, and she worked almost every day while her four sons were at school. Val was consciously employing the traditional homemaker's techniques – crochet, knitting, mending and rug-making – along with soft sculpture techniques she had developed to enhance the themes of her work. These ranged from motherhood and maidens to marriage and men.

Val is now prepared to be labelled as a feminist artist. She wants her work to be enigmatic, to ask questions rather than to give answers. She chooses materials and techniques to suit the message. After the large and difficult-to-deal-with works in 'Stuffing On', Val is enjoying making a carefully constructed series of smaller works. She uses fabrics because she just 'knows' how to make them work, but also because fabrics, and 'womanly' skills such as stitching, embroidering and felting, help to tell the story.

Tray cloths

I met Val when I was teaching in New Zealand, at an exhibition of extraordinary work entitled 'Do Make/ Make Do'. The exhibition was about Val's response to the dreadful earthquake in Christchurch, New Zealand in February 2011. I remember a washing line of tiny jumpers and cardigans, some beautiful sofas and crazy caravans as well beautiful sculptures – all tiny. I was particularly taken with the tray cloths (these were not tiny) that were exhibited on the wall. Taking something that has already been beautifully embroidered and then stitching into it again in your own style takes courage. Val obviously had strong feelings about what she wanted to say.

Val comments: 'After the earthquakes I felt in the role of someone who wanted to help, but was unable to make any practical difference. I felt unable to act, except to make symbolic sources of comfort. The food, the tents and jerseys relate to my response to all disaster. When I am stuck with what to do for a sick friend, how to say thanks, I think "I shall knit." Other folk bake.
'The tray cloths are a link between myself and the woman who originally stitched them. I started to stitch them aged about 9 and have gone back to add to them over the years. I think, as I stitch, "What would these women have chosen to say/ stitch were they given the freedom that I now enjoy?" I stitched these cloths with a free hand, and a free mind, unlike the woman who carefully worked on the original tray cloth. Chain stitch, blanket stitch, lazy daisy, feather stitch and cross-stitch: traditional stitches have all helped to tell many stories beside my own.'

Val now lives in Picton, New Zealand, creating her marvellous work and teaching various textile-related workshops. She enjoys encouraging beginners, helping everyone to experiment and have fun. I highly recommend that you visit her website (see page 120) – it is very amusing!

RIGHT *Role Models I Wish I Had Had.* Hand embroidery on a linen cloth Val originally made as a child of nine or ten.

Helen McKenna

Helen has stitched from a very young age. At first she stitched clothes for her dolls, then for herself, and then for others as the years progressed. Quite late in life, Helen decided to acquire some qualifications and enrolled on Part 1 of a City and Guilds Institute Fashion course. She loved going to night school, where she learned how to make patterns and alter purchased patterns to fit, and of course lots of sewing techniques which are still relevant today. Helen went on to take

Part 2 and then the City and Guilds Creative Embroidery course, Parts 1 and 2. Next, she decided to study for a degree in Contemporary Applied Arts. During the degree course, Helen started to use constructed textiles in her work, employing vintage fabrics, tulle, silks, dyed and embroidered tablecloths, and fleece. However, she hadn't really developed her own style and as the final year approached, panic set in. Helen has always loved embroidered shoes and decided to write her dissertation on the subject. She also began to incorporate them into her work.

RIGHT *Pink Shoes* by Helen McKenna. Decorated with felt and net embellishments.

Shoes

It wasn't viable for Helen to actually make shoes, so she started to embellish satin wedding shoes, scouring charity shops far and wide to find them. For her degree show, Helen bought some that had been worn in a fashion show from a local bridal shop. A trip to Buenos Aires provided inspiration in the form of architecture, flower stalls selling roses and gerberas, railings, and the paintings of Frida Kahlo. Madeira sponsored Helen for the last year of her degree, providing most of the threads for her show. In 2007, Helen was a finalist in the Hand and Lock embroidery competition. She made a jacket and embellished some satin wedding boots based on Victorian mourning clothes. This was the same year she gained a first class honours degree in Contemporary Applied Arts.

ABOVE *Yellow and Green Shoes.* Decorated with felt, vintage tablecloth embroideries, pleated net and finished with beads.

The influences of South America, Frida Kahlo and the Day of the Dead festival can still be seen in Helen's work today. Most of her work involves the use of an embellisher machine (a machine that looks like a sewing machine, with a foot that has five needle-felting needles to 'felt' fibres together) to construct fabric. This is then decorated with machine stitching, hand stitching, beads and buttons and used to cover satin shoes. She uses a rubber glue to attach the fabric to the shoes, covering the shoe first and then the heel. A textured yarn fills in any gaps around the base and heel of the shoe. Dyed, embroidered tablecloths provide the lining: Helen searches in charity shops to find these, and prefers them to be stained so she doesn't feel so guilty when chopping them up. Once the glue is dry, Helen further embellishes the shoes using tulle, beads, machine-stitched wire and dyed felt.

Helen is a member of Trident Textiles. The group has exhibited at various venues across the UK.

Log-cabin cushion

The log-cabin design is a traditional style of patchwork, and my favourite way of creating patchwork. You only need a few pins and there is no need to tack any fabrics in place. A cushion cover can be made within an hour. All you need are strips of fabric, a background to stitch on to, a sewing machine, an iron and an ironing board. I like to work in a random fashion, using fabric strips as they come to hand. If you wish to create a pattern, you could use the same fabrics for every second and fourth strip. Check that the strips of fabric are long enough before you start to stitch them to the background. I like to work in tones of one colour, mixing patterned and plain fabrics.

It can be daunting to start a patchwork project if you haven't had a lot of experience, but there are many products that can help, such as fabrics with grids printed on them to help you line up fabric pieces and keep them square. Quickscreen Square was used for this project (Quickscreen Triangle is also available for use with hexagonal and lozenge shapes). It is a washable, sew-in product so doesn't need to be removed and acts as your backing fabric. There is an iron-on version called Quilter's Grid which is also washable and need not be removed. All these products are supported by the Vilene website listed on page 123.

You will need
• **Fabrics for the patchwork**
• **40 x 40cm (16 x 16in) cushion pad**
• **Backing fabric, such as a firm calico (washed and ironed), for the cushion front: 44 x 44cm (17½ x 17½in) or use gridded fabric as described above.**
• **Fabric, such as a firm patterned cotton matching one of your strips, for the cushion back: 34 x 40cm (13½ x 16in) and 22 x 40cm (8¾ x 16in)**
• **Sewing machine**
• **Iron and ironing board**
• **Matching machine sewing thread**

RIGHT Finished cushion front and back, showing the two overlapped sections that create the 'envelope' openings.

1   2

Instructions

1 Select your fabrics. I prefer to use firm cottons for patchwork. You could use synthetics, but they can slip about a bit. I have chosen fabrics in tones of one colour but there is nothing wrong with using many different colours. I raided my ragbag to find this selection. If necessary, unpick any garments and if fabrics are creased, iron them.

2 Tear or cut the fabric into strips at least 4cm (1½in) wide. Log cabin can be made with any width of strip from 12mm (½in) to any width you think would look good. However, if this is all new to you, work with strips that are easy to handle. If you are cutting the strips, make sure that you cut on the straight grain of the fabric. Fabric will tear down the straight grain; I always tear my fabrics for log-cabin piecing, as it is much faster than cutting and you know that the strips with be on the straight grain.

3 If you are not using the suggested size of cushion pad, measure the pad and add 2cm (¾in) all the way round. Cut a piece of backing fabric or Quickscreen Square to this measurement.

4

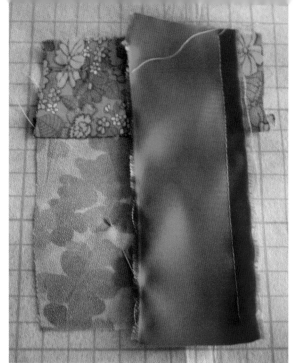

5

Tip
Every time you come to stitch a new fabric strip, position your work ready to stitch, put the presser foot down, hold both threads down with your left hand and turn the hand wheel towards you until the needle is in your work. This way, you will know that there is enough thread to make the first stitch. There is nothing more annoying than the thread pulling out of the needle because it is not long enough. This advice was given to me many years ago; it is a good habit to get into and saves so much time.

6

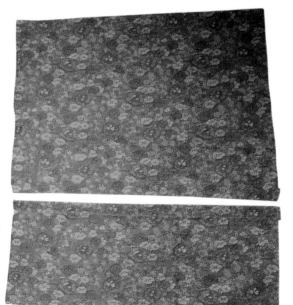

7

4 Choose a fabric to go in the centre of the cushion. A 9cm (3½in) square is a good size, though it can be bigger. Pin this in the centre of the backing fabric. Take one of the fabric strips and stitch it, right-side down, along one side of the middle square, 1cm (⅜in) from the edge. Fold the strip back over to show the right side and press the seam with the iron.

5 Continue adding strips, working in a clockwise direction. Press each seam open as you go: this will give a sharp finish to your work.

6 As you continue to work in a clockwise direction, you will need longer and longer strips of fabric. Do check that each strip you are about to use is long enough.

7 When the cushion front has reached the correct size, and with an equal number of strips on all sides of the middle square, press all the seams. You can then make the cushion back. Hem both rectangles along one of the long edges (you have a 2cm/ ¾in allowance). Press the hems.

8 Place the cushion front right-side up. Lay the wider rectangle of the cushion back, right-side down on top, matching the top and side edges, with the hem approximately three-quarters of the way down the length of the cushion. Lay the other rectangle over this, right-side down, matching the bottom and side edges of the front and overlapping the hems by approximately 8cm (3¼in). Make sure all the edges are level and lined up. Pin together and then stitch with a 2cm (¾in) seam, making sure you remove the pins as you stitch. Trim the seam allowance to 1cm (⅜in) and cut carefully cut across the corners, leaving 1cm (⅜in) of seam. This will give you sharp corners when you turn the cover out.

9 Turn the cover right side out, making sure the corners are pushed out, and press the seams. Insert the cushion pad.

BELOW These cushion covers are made from strips of lamé fabrics, Thai silk, brocade and sari fabric.

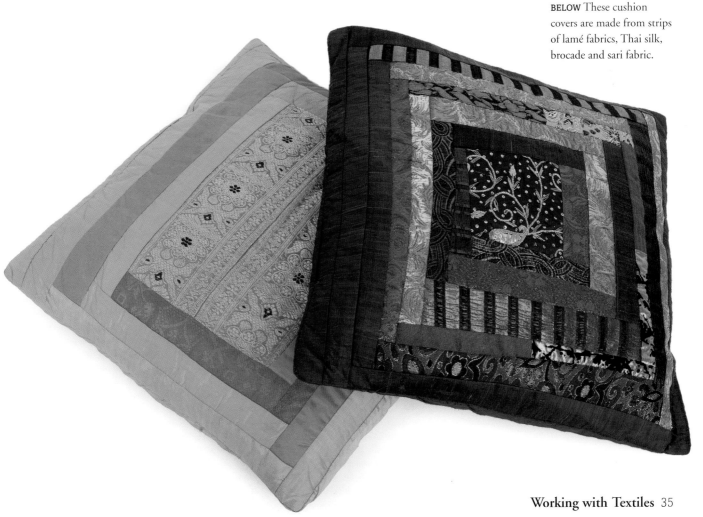

Knitted fabrics

Knitted fabrics are great fun to play with. If you can find hand-knitted woollen garments, they can usually be unpicked and re-knitted, or the yarn can be used for weaving or stitching. Woollen garments can be felted and then made into other items. Synthetic and cotton knitted garments can be made into all kinds of projects from bags to patchwork cushions, coats, curtains or even toy pigs!

Old T-shirts in bright colours can be turned into dresses, new and more complicated T-shirts, bags or book covers. T-shirts can also be cut into strips, knotted together and then knitted to create yet another fabric. Because knitted fabrics stretch, you will probably need an interfacing or stabilizer to stop the fabric you are working with from stretching. However, you can also try pulling and stretching knitted fabric as you stitch – it can create a fabulous buckled and wavy effect.

Michelle Edinburgh

Michelle began making sock monkeys after taking part in an online workshop with artist and art therapist Katarina Thorsen. Kat lives in Canada and uses 'sock monkey therapy' with at-risk youth. A sock monkey is so much more than a toy: it is a talking point, a therapeutic aid in an internal journey of self-transformation.

Michelle was instantly captivated by the idea of the sock monkey and began making them with young people and adults in her work as an art therapist. She watched as their creations became invested with the pain, joy and drama of their inner lives. Made using only a single pair of socks, some stuffing, thread and buttons, a sock monkey is a chimera of bits and bobs from the artist's life and the art-room floor. A plain and simple sock monkey can be just as beautiful as a decorative and embellished one. Students embellish their sock monkeys with all sorts of things. Some have added lavender to the stuffing and once a precious stone, believed to have healing qualities, was placed inside a special monkey for a sick relative. You really can let your imagination run riot with a sock monkey.

Michelle has noticed that students never fail to be surprised at the amazing characters they create from a silly old sock. Her students range from the chronically ill, to a 2-year-old and on to her 94-year-old grandmother. One student was virtually bedridden for a year but is now up and about and on the mend. Michelle is certain that the fun of sourcing the materials from what she could find and sewing them into a little character has helped her to focus on something other than her fears and her pain.

LEFT Sock Monkeys Rose
(left) and Emmeline (right).

Sock-monkey therapy

Emmaline, on the right, is half-warrior and half-goddess and was created for a 'Guess the name of the sock monkey' competition during a charity fundraiser. Her body is formed from a pair of stripy socks, and her hair is made from recycled silk strands from old saris. With her appliquéd red heart, she is a great character and went to a great home (mine: I guessed the name). Rose, on the left, is made from a pair of Solmate socks, which are produced from recycled cotton such as old T-shirts. She is rich in colour and texture. Rose has two buttons forming each eye, because Michelle loved all the buttons that she had to hand and couldn't decide which to choose! Rose also has recycled sari yarn for her hair.

Sissy Rooney

I was first introduced to sock pigs and jumper owls when I had a stand opposite Sissy at the Design and Technology show at the NEC in Birmingham. Her use of recycled textiles was very innovative and exciting, but it was the pigs that stole my heart. I was impressed with Sissy's energy and commitment to what she was doing and knew that I needed to include her in this book.

Sissy runs a very successful business in the north-west of England called Street Style Surgery, which aspires to be the number-one provider of fashion and education workshops in the UK. It runs creative workshops for young people, which educate, stimulate and encourage personal growth so that participants can discover hidden talents and unlock their potential. Sissy's goal is to show them that it is possible to make a living doing something they love and feel passionate about.

When cutting knitted fabrics, care needs to be taken to stop the knitted fabric from unravelling, though it's not too much of a problem with fine machine knitted fabrics such as the ones used here. To make absolutely certain, edges can be overlocked and cut at the same time. If you don't have an overlocking machine, a zig-zag machine stitch would help stop the edges fraying.

The sock pigs are made from an ankle sock. The heel is used for the nose and the ears. The rest of the sock from the heel up is used for the body. The ears are stitched to the body first, the body is then stuffed with a fine polyester wadding such as Deco Wadding. The heel is then slipped into the ankle elastic to create the nose and hand stitched into place with small stitches in a self-coloured thread. The feet are created by taking a section of the body with a little stuffing and running a line of stitching around the length of the foot.

The owls on the opposite page are made from jumper material (left) and an old synthetic sock (right). The body of the owl is a small rectangular cushion stuffed with wadding. The wings are then added as is the eye shape. Your owl can then have button and/or bead eyes. The beaks have been made from a small triangle of felt, but a piece of jumper or t-shirt would be fine.

LEFT The puppets can be decorated with buttons for nostrils and beads for eyes. You could give them hair by stitching in strands of wool. It's up to you!

Jayne Routley

Jayne Routley is a keen felt-maker and textile artist based in Brighton. She exhibits and sells her work through the Brighton Open Houses twice a year and has work in several private collections. Jayne has been featured in *Hot Textiles*, *Experimental Textiles* and *Layered Textiles* and is a founding member of the exhibiting textile group Threads. As with most of us, Jayne is now very interested in the sustainability of her work and enjoys working with all manner of textiles.

Jumper bag

Many of you will have spilled food, paint or dye on a well-loved jumper and thought it irredeemable. Well, think again… whether it's machine- or hand-knitted, knitted fabric can be cut and stitched just like any other fabric. When cutting into knitted fabric that has not been felted you need to stop it fraying somehow. An overlocker would be the best choice of machine to use or you could use a zig-zag stitch on a basic domestic sewing machine instead. If you prefer to work by hand you could over-stitch the raw edges. If sewing together by machine, a walking foot will help you keep the fabric flat and not stretch it as you sew. This bag was made from an old jumper. The arms have been used to make the handle and the neck has been used to make the pocket. If you create a bag out of knitted fabric, line it with a firm fabric to stop the bag from stretching.

ABOVE AND RIGHT The jumper that became a bag, and the finished bag. You can have great fun applying unusual shaped pockets.

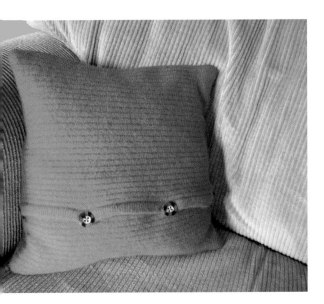

Sue Culligan

Sue Culligan lives in France and runs knitting and crochet retreats and workshops from her home in the beautiful Charente Maritime district. She is a very experienced knitter, a pattern editor for *Knitting Magazine* and has written four books on knitting. Sue trained at Brighton Art College and has always had a great eye for texture and colour.

Sue's cushion would be great fun to make up as a group project, with each member bringing in a jumper to deconstruct and turn into a cushion. Parts of different jumpers could also be shared to make random-coloured cushions.

Recycled cardigan cushion cover

This cover is designed for a 40 x 40cm (16 x 16in) cushion pad, but measurements can be changed to fit any cushion pad – just remember to add on a 2cm (¾in) seam allowance all around.

You will need
• 40 x 40cm (16 x 16in) cushion pad
• Old cardigan knitted in pure wool or alpaca, with washing instructions stating it should only be hand-washed
• Buttons (if not using the buttons from your original garment)

Instructions

1 Remove the buttons from the cardigan and machine-wash with detergent at 40°C. This should be sufficient to matt the fibres without causing too much shrinkage. If the knitted stitches are still clearly defined, wash again at 60°C. Stretch into shape and allow to dry naturally.

2 Cut out a square from the back of the cardigan measuring 42 x 42cm (16½ x16½in). This will form the back of the cushion.

3 From the front of the cardigan, cut a rectangle that measures 42cm (16½in) along the buttonhole band x 32cm (12½in). Make sure you cut it so that the end buttonholes are spaced at an equal distance from each cut edge. This will be Front A.

4 From the other cardigan front, cut a rectangle that measures 42cm (16½in) along the button band x 23cm (9in). This will be Front B.

5 Lay the cushion back face up, then place Front A face down on this, matching the top and side edges. Lay Front B face down, matching the bottom and side edges with the cushion front so that it overlaps the piece with the buttonholes by 11cm (4½in).

6 Pin the pieces of fabric together, then machine-stitch (use a large stitch setting on the machine to prevent puckering) all the way around 2cm (¾in) in from the edge. Cut off the excess fabric close to the seam so that it isn't too bulky.

7 Turn right-side out and sew the buttons in place to correspond with the buttonholes. Insert the cushion pad.

8 If desired, the cushion could be decorated with hand stitch or appliqué.

Working with Paper

Working with paper

Paper is produced by pressing together moist fibres, typically cellulose pulp derived from wood, rags or grasses, and drying them into flexible sheets. Paper has been used for thousands of years and we are still finding new ways to make it, new products to make it from, and new ways to work with it.

Whilst paper is not a textile, I cannot leave it out of this book as we can use it for so many textile techniques – from quilting to collage – and it is a wonderful material to stitch into. If you wish to stitch into thin papers by hand or machine, you may need to stabilize the paper with a fine iron-on interfacing. This will not change the 'handle' of the paper too much but will stop it from tearing. When machine-stitching paper, whether in single sheets or many layers, always use a long stitch length, as the machine needle will create perforations and if these are too close together, your work may fall apart.

If you buy paper from a shop, you will be able to choose from commercial man-made papers or handmade papers. Commercial papers tend to be smooth and uniform in texture with hard, cut edges, whereas handmade papers can be thick and fibrous and have an uneven surface with frayed or uneven edges.

Different types of paper will tear in different ways. Because of the structure of handmade papers, they can be difficult to tear evenly. Use a 'wet' tear to help with this. On a flat surface, fold the paper along the line you wish to tear, then dip a paintbrush in water and run it along the fold until the fold is quite damp. On a flat surface, support one side of the paper firmly with one hand, and gently pull the other side of the folded paper until it tears along the fold. You should achieve a beautiful 'frayed' edge as the fibres pull apart. This technique is very useful when making concertina books.

However you don't have to rely on purchased paper. There are so many types of paper around us that are available to play with, wherever you live in the world – just look at the envelopes that are posted through your letterbox, gift wrappings that arrive on presents or old calendars. I am particularly fond of handwritten envelopes. In these days of digital technology and social networking it seems all the more precious when a friend or loved one has taken the time to put pen to paper. I save all handwritten envelopes that I receive – birthdays and Christmas are obviously bumper times. As with all papers, these envelopes can be coloured with watered-down paint.

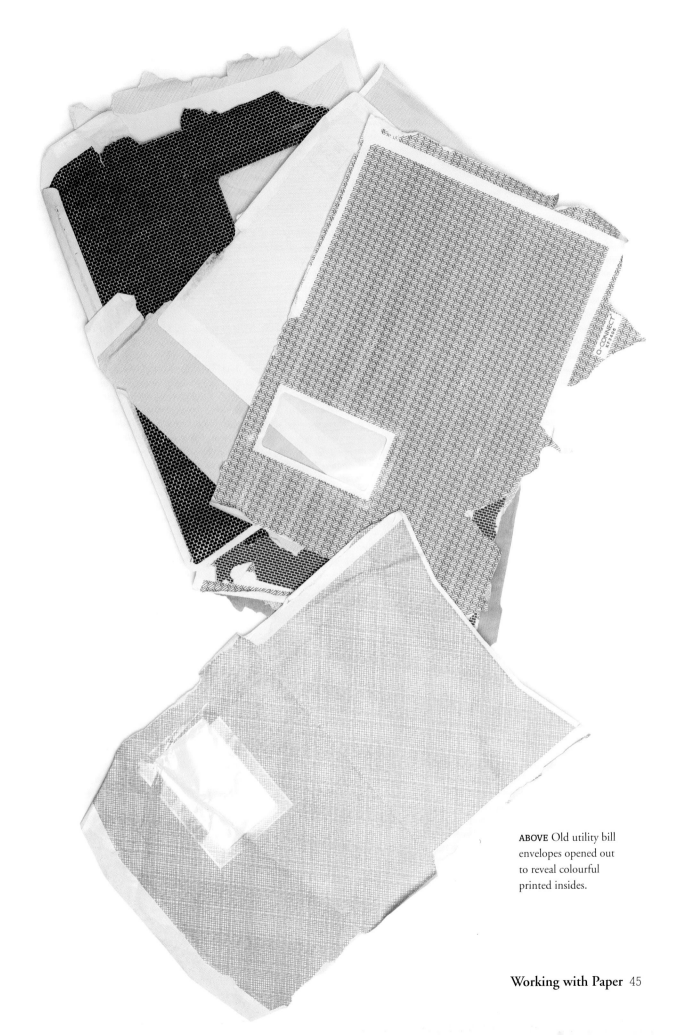

ABOVE Old utility bill envelopes opened out to reveal colourful printed insides.

Envelope collage of 'Raggs

and 'Dolly' my puppy!

Sarah Hawkins

Have a look inside the envelope that your utility or bank information comes in – it will probably have coloured patterns inside. Sarah Hawkins has made good use of these. She is a textile artist and dog groomer and has a passion for bearded collies. She even collects their hair after grooming sessions and felts it.

Sarah created these collaged portraits of her beloved 'beardies' from the inside of envelopes. Simply by tearing envelopes and using the different tones of colour to show light and dark area of the dogs' faces, Sarah has given life to Dolly in the pink collage and Raggs in the blue one. These pieces were part of Sarah's sketchbook on my Experimental Textiles course several years ago, and when I was commissioned to write this book I knew I wanted to include them.

ABOVE *Raggs* on the left and *Dolly* on the right. Simple but effective collages in Sarah's course folder. All you need is old envelopes and paste.
OPPOSITE *Dolly* was created using old envelopes and wrapping paper.

Photographs

I have boxes of old photographs of students' work and instead of throwing them out, I have decided to start stitching into them and then printing on the stitched images. Such work can be finished with acrylic wax or non-yellowing floor varnish. The sample shown here would make a fabulous book cover.

In order to make a good background to print on, it is best to collect photographs into groups of one or two colours. Colours that are too contrasting will be too distracting and you won't see the print. Tear or cut the photographs into strips and then sort into colour-coordinated groups. I like to hand-stitch into the photographs, but you can just as easily use machine stitch. If you choose to machine stitch, use a long stitch or you will create too many perforations and your work may fall apart. Once you have finished your work it will be quite firm. If further reinforcement is required, use an iron-on interfacing.

Printing onto paper feels less scary, less permanent even, than printing onto fabric. Have fun experimenting with all manner of printing blocks – commercial wooden blocks, any you have made yourself, even a carved half of a potato. It is not necessary to use a roller (brayer) to apply the paint if you don't have one; a wide paintbrush can work just as well. Just apply the paint thinly. Always test the amount of paint you need on your printing block on a spare piece of paper before you launch into your finished masterpiece. I tend to use acrylic paints for printing as they are a good consistency for printing. If you find the paint you are using is a bit thick, just water it down slightly. One handy tip for printing – always print onto a slightly padded surface. An old towel or blanket covered in an old sheet would work well. This will give your print better definition.

However, in the age of digital photography, fewer and fewer of us are choosing to print our images. Indeed, paper may be the last medium you think of printing images on as there are now many pre-treated fabric sheets available that can be fed through a printer and these provide exciting possibilities. To make a fabric firm enough to put though your ink-jet printer, iron one or two layers of Fuse-n-Tear onto your fabric and cut accurately to A4 or A3 size depending on the size of your printer. You can feel if your fabric is stiff enough with one sheet of Fuse-n-Tear; if not, add another. Then feed your stiffened fabric through your printer. Fuse-n-Tear is an iron-on, peel-off stabiliser for stitching stretch fabrics but is also very useful for stiffening fabrics to print onto, and as it is a peel-off product, you can re use the Fuse-n-Tear until the adhesive is used up.

It is now possible to buy packs of pre-treated fabrics for your ink-jet printer. There are many choices including ones that will also iron-on. Do a quick search on the Internet and you will be amazed at the choice. There are also several pre-coating media that you can paint onto fabric to aid the printing process on fabric and paper – inkAID is my favourite. There are several videos on YouTube to help you understand how to use a pre-coat. It has never been easier to print images from your computer – have fun!

ABOVE *Printed sample*. Photographs of rag rugs torn and
sorted into colour tones then hand stitched together. I chose
to print with a pink that appeared in the blue-grey image.
Using a toning colour to print with, rather than a
contrasting one, will help the print to 'bleed' in and out.

Newspaper

One of the most popular workshops I run includes the use of another readily available type of paper – newspaper. When torn and layered, it creates a fabulous surface on which to stitch and print. You can colour the newspaper before you use it. I use old newspapers to protect my table when I am painting and dyeing products. Because I use gorgeous metallic paints and brightly coloured dyes, the newspaper starts to build up a wonderful random layer of colour. I dry out the papers and keep reusing them until they are covered in colour. You will not necessarily have the time to do this as it takes a few months, but you can create a similar look by sploshing on any or all of the paints and dyes you have. It is great fun, but you need to allow a lot of space for the papers to dry separately, as two painted surfaces will stick together.

You might also like to make a feature of certain words and images that appear in newspapers, to add a further dimension to your work. Consider international newspapers too: bring interesting examples home from your travels or find them in supermarkets and newsagents at home.

Even the pages of old novels are suitable for this type of work. Thousands of books are given to charity shops and recycling centres every week. There has never been a better time to source old papers.

1

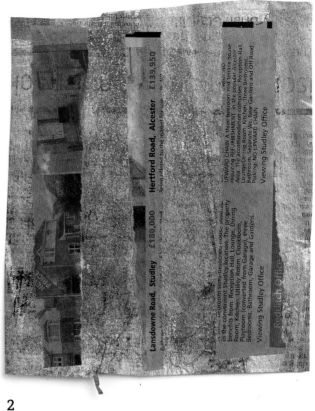

2

'Pretties' and backgrounds

This project combines newspaper and sparkly embellishments with repeats and tearing and layering to create exciting surfaces: the self-explanatory 'pretties' and backgrounds. You can go on to stitch and print on them. Please take care, when ironing, to have baking parchment underneath *and* on top of your work *every* time you iron it. The strips of leftover 'pretties' can be used for all kinds of decoration, for example you can apply them to greetings cards or even use them to cover a box canvas (see page 54).

You will need
• Newspaper sploshed with paint and dye (see left) cut into 15cm (6in) squares (you will need at least 10 in contrasting colours)
• 50cm (½yd) Bondaweb, cut into 6 pieces
• Roll of baking parchment
• Iron and ironing board
• All manner of sparkly embellishments – gilding flakes, flat sequins, glitter, mica flakes, dot jewels
• Paper scissors

Instructions

1 Take a square of newspaper and lay it on an A4-sized piece of baking parchment. Cut a square of Bondaweb to fit just inside the edges. Lay the Bondaweb on the newspaper with the rough side facing downwards (this is the sticky side). Cover with another A4-sized piece of baking parchment and iron with a hot iron for 30 seconds. Once cold, remove the baking parchment and backing paper from the Bondaweb. This forms the first background.

2 Iron three or four strips of torn newspaper on to the background, leaving space in between the strips.

3

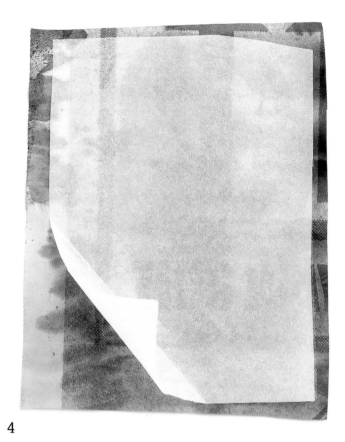

4

5

6

3 In the spaces between the strips of newspaper, sprinkle (delicately) some of the sparkly embellishments. Take care to avoid the newspaper strips. Cover with baking parchment and iron for 30 seconds. Remove the baking parchment when cold. You now have a 'pretty'!

4 Repeating step 1, create another background square of deecorated newspaper fused to Bondaweb.

5 Now tear the 'pretty' into irregular strips. Iron three or four of these strips on to the new background, making sure you lay baking

parchment on top before you iron it. You will have some strips left over: put them to one side for another project. Sprinkle more sparkly embellishments in the spaces between the 'pretty' strips. Cover with baking parchment and iron for 30 seconds. Remove the baking parchment when cold. You now have another 'pretty'.

6 This second 'pretty' can then be torn into strips and ironed on to yet another background. The process can be repeated several times until the work is quite thick. It is important to only work with one pretty at a time. Once you have a 'pretty', you make another background that becomes a 'pretty', so you make another background that becomes a 'pretty'…

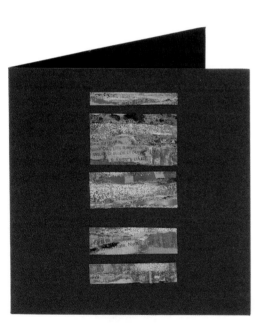
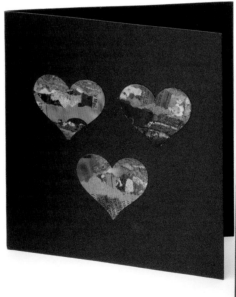

Cards

Put your remaining 'pretty' strips to good use by creating unique greetings cards. Simply cut them into smaller pieces or into different shapes and glue to the front of a card.

ABOVE Black card folded to create greetings cards and decorated with leftover 'pretty' strips.

Covering a canvas

'Pretties' are great for making striking pieces of art to hang on the wall. All you need is a small box canvas, available from art shops, to work on. You can add all manner of decoration but you might not need much more glitz as the 'pretties' are already sparkly.

You will need
• Box canvas. I used a 15 x 15cm (6 x 6in) canvas for this project but you can use any size. You just need paper to cover the canvas.
• Newspaper sploshed with paint and dye (see page 50)
• Wallpaper paste
• Up to 30cm (12in) Bondaweb, depending on your canvas size
• Water-based paints
• Roll of baking parchment
• Iron and ironing board
• Iron-on gemstones
• Gold heat-transfer foil
• Leftover 'pretties'
• Foil glue
• Paper scissors
• Acrylic wax

Instructions

1 Tear the painted newspaper into strips and glue them to the canvas with wallpaper paste, covering the canvas completely. Leave to dry.

2 Paint the Bondaweb with water-based paints. The paint needs to be thin (as a rule, water down by half). Leave it to dry. Take the painted Bondaweb and iron it onto the front of your paper covered canvas. If you are unsure, there is a video on my blog (see page 123).

3 Cut strips of leftover 'pretties' and iron them on to the painted Bondaweb, again using baking parchment.

4 You can embellish the canvas further. I have added iron-on gemstones, and used gold heat-transfer foil at the sides of the canvas, pressing it on to foil glue. (Foil glue is glue that stays tacky to the touch and heat-transfer foil can be applied to it by pressing the foil, colour-side up, on to the surface of the glue.)

5 When the canvas is finished, seal it with three layers of acrylic wax.

Veronica Wells

The piece shown above, by Veronica Wells, shows another way of combining coloured newspaper and Bondaweb successfully. Veronica is interested in the interpretation of texture in textiles but also in the use of layers and text and lettering, so that meanings are both hidden and revealed.

I met Veronica on a course I was running at Bobby Britnell's studio in Shropshire. The course was based on layering newspaper with painted Bondaweb. As you can see, her use of colour and her sensitive hand stitching produced something quite stunning. Dyed and painted newspapers were torn and layered with painted Bondaweb and ironed between baking parchment to create a fascinating surface on which to print and stitch.

The course also included learning how to print on Solufleece (a water-soluble stabilizer for machine embroidery). It was stretched in an embroidery ring and block printed with a fern motif. The printed design was then free machine stitched in a similar colour to the one used to make the print. Next, the Solufleece was dissolved around the stitched design and carefully hand-stitched to the printed leaf sample to give an extra dimension. See page 8 for a step-by-step explanantion of this process.

It is not absolutely necessary to use free-machine embroidery to create a similar sample. Simple hand stitches could also be used to great effect: the stitched design would just be less three-dimensional.

ABOVE Leaf sample. A beautiful piece of work incorporating torn strips of newspaper, print and free-machine-embroidered leaf shapes.

Kim Thittichai

I live in Brighton, on the south coast of England. It is a fabulous place to live, with all the shops and entertainments, but I also have to share it with many other people, including thousands of visitors to the city. Because of this, I rarely visit the seafront in the summer: it is just too crowded. In the winter it is a different story – more space, a different light – wonderful. We have two piers in between Brighton and Hove. The Palace Pier, full of bright plastic, lights and a funfair, and the poor old West Pier, which has more or less fallen into the sea. The structure of this stunning building is still visible, but more and more is being washed away every year. I have always loved the patterns formed by the exposed steels, particularly the crossed steels that support the main structure. Over the years these crossed steels have got covered with all kinds of detritus, plastic bags, brightly coloured nylon ropes and fishing nets.

This was the inspiration for a piece of work that I started as a student on a summer school three years ago. As a tutor, it is very important to keep topping up your learning and working with tutors who stretch you, and for this I turn to the Textile Study Group.

This body of work uses large-scale herringbone stitch to represent the crossed steels, and a faux chenille made from distressed newspaper for the ragged detritus. The newspaper areas have been ironed on to painted Bondaweb; the Bondaweb and newspaper have been

decorated in areas with embossing powders and gold and silver micro beads.

Embossing powders are used for the craft of card-making, along with rubber stamps and special embossing ink pads. The powder sticks to the image that has been printed with the ink. It is heated gently with a heat gun and becomes shiny and molten, cooling down to show the printed shape. I use a glue stick to stop the embossing powders from blowing away when I

heat them with a heat gun. Micro beads are tiny little beads that don't have a hole in them. They can be sprinkled into wet glue, paint and molten embossing powders – with care. They give the impression of sand.

ABOVE AND LEFT *Crossed Steels*. Once the newspaper pieces were completed, they were stuck onto canvases pre-covered in strips of newspaper. The entire piece was then sprayed with polyurathane varnish.

Newspaper faux chenille project

There are many different types of medium- to heavy-weight interfacings – until now 'pelmet Vilene' has been the most popular choice, a medium-weight sew-in interfacing that is very useful for small boxes and book covers. However, there are new interfacings now available from Freudenberg Vilene that are iron-on and therefore can speed up the creative process. These iron-on interfacings can be decorated with heat-transfer foils; glitter, sequins and gilding flakes as you would decorate painted Bondaweb (see page 10).

Decovil 1 Light is a fusible, non-woven interfacing that is thinner and more drapable than pelmet Vilene, excellent for book covers and soft bags and it has a lovely leathery feel to it. Decovil 1 is a medium weight iron-on interfacing and is perfect for heavier bags, belts and soft bags. This is also leather-like.

S133 is the heavyweight iron-on interfacing. It is very stiff and wonderful for larger boxes and vessels – anything that you don't want to sag in the middle.

Any of theses interfacings can used to back newspaper faux chenille to create three-dimensional projects. The individual project will dictate which weight of iron-interfacing you choose. All interfacings can be cut with a knife, scissors or with a die-cutting machine.

You will need
- Old painted and dyed newspapers
- Sewing machine
- Polyester organza
- Iron-on interfacing cut to size. Soft – Decovil 1 light, Medium – Decovil 1, Hard/heavy – S133
- An iron and baking parchment
- Your pre-cut and coloured box/bag shape of iron-on interfacing. In this project I have used Decovil 1 Light, cut with a Big Shot Pro die cutting machine.
- Plastikote Kystal Clear varnish aerosol spray (always use spray outside)
- Suede brush or washing up brush
- Roll of baking parchment

Tips

I would recommend stitching the layers with a long stitch length – no 4 on most sewing machines. The needle will create perforations and when you start to distress the 'chenille' your work will fall apart if you have a used a short stitch length.

You need to stitch the length of the layers in the same direction; turning the layers as you stitch will create a puckered effect. Cut your thread every time you get to the end of a line of stitch and go back to the top. Always make sure there is enough thread to make the first stitch when you start to stitch – again, there are few things more irritating than the needle becoming unthreaded. A tip is to hold the top and bobbin thread down on the needle plate with your left hand then turn the handwheel towards you until your needle is in your work. This is good habit to get into every time you start to stitch – there will always be enough thread for your first stitch and there is less strain on your machine.

To colour the iron-on interfacing, use a very dilute solution of acrylic paint (one third paint to two thirds water). If the paint is too thick it will stop the glue from being heat activated – you need more of a colour wash than a thick layer of paint. It can take 24 hours to dry so make sure you paint it in advance.

Use whichever cutting tool suits you – there is a special faux chenille rotary cutter available, but do bear in mind that cutting layers of newspaper will blunt your tools and may make them useless on fabrics.

FAR RIGHT A pocket bag made with the faux chenille.

1 Cut four sheets of painted and/or dyed newspaper and three pieces of polyester organza to size. Layer the polyester organza between the sheets of newspaper, ending with newspaper on top. Pin the layers together so they don't slip about. Stitch lines roughly 2cm apart. The narrower the spaces between the lines of stitch, the more difficult it can be to cut between them. Remove the pins as you stitch.

2 Once you have stitched all the lines right across your layers you can iron your layers onto your pre-cut and coloured iron-on interfacing. The sticky side of the iron-on interfacing is the shiny side. Make sure you know which side is which before you iron your layers onto the interfacing. Using baking parchment underneath and on top of your work, iron the interfacing onto the back of your layers. Take two minutes to iron the project slowly and then leave to cool. The heat has to get through the baking parchment and the iron-on interfacing to melt the glue. The thicker the iron-interfacing the longer you need to iron your project. Once cool, check the interfacing is stuck to the newspaper then remove the baking parchment. Trim the newspaper layers to match the iron-on interfacing.

3 Carefully cut through all the layers except the interfacing. Distress the cut edges with a firm brush, taking care of the edges of your work in case they pull away from the interfacing. One you have finished distressing your work, spray (outside! – the fumes are vicious) with a clear varnish to seal the work. Your project can then be folded up to create you bag or box and finished to your taste.

If you are making a more complicated box project you may wish to decorate only certain areas of the box with faux chenille as the thick layers can interfere with the folding process.

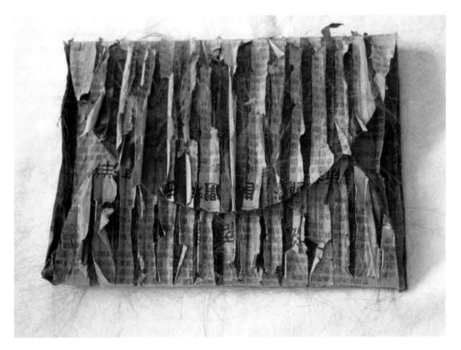

Newspaper boxes

Decorated newspaper can be ironed on to medium- or heavy weight interfacings to create boxes or bags, depending on how stiff the interfacing is. For the boxes and brooches shown here, I used the very heavy Vilene iron-on interfacing S133. This is the heaviest iron-interfacing normally used in the soft-furnishing trade. The stiff, card-like interfacing is light in weight, excellent for objects that need to stand as in boxes and taller vessels and is also great for making jewellery. The heat-activated glue side is easily identifiable as it is the shiny side.

Once the decorated newspaper was ironed on to the interfacing, I cut it to shape with a die-cutting machine. This type of interfacing can be cut with scissors or a scalpel, but it is much easier if you use a die-cutting machine. Finally, I sealed my boxes by painting them with acrylic wax.

Die-cutting is like using a pastry cutter. A hand-operated die-cutting machine uses steel die shapes to cut through a wide range of materials quickly and easily. It will give a sharp, professional-looking finish. A die-cutting machine can emboss and texturize many materials, including cardstock, paper, construction paper, fabric, faux fur, felt, foil, heat and shrink plastic, leather, wood, poly foam, self-adhesive rubber (for making rubber stamps), sheet magnet, sponge, static cling vinyl and thin craft metal.

BELOW AND RIGHT Heavy iron-on interfacing decorated with torn strips of 'pretties' (see pages 51–53).

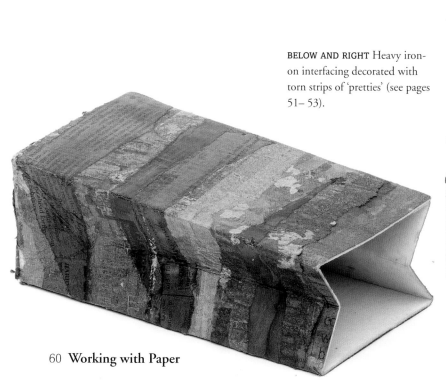

Newspaper brooches

Brooches can be made in the same way as the newspaper boxes. When you have created the shape, you just stick a brooch pin on the back and finally seal the front and back of the brooch with acrylic wax.

You will need
• **Leftover newspaper 'pretties' (see page 51)**
• **Enough S133 interfacing for your project**
• **Baking parchment**
• **Acrylic wax and paintbrush**
• **Brooch back if making brooches**
• **Iron and a stable working surface**

To cut your project:
A die-cutting machine or
scalpel and cutting mat or
paper scissors

Instructions

If using a die-cutting machine, cut the S133 to the size of the die – the ones used here were a 30cm (12in) die for the boxes and a 15cm (6in) for the brooches.

If cutting with a scalpel, roughly cut the S133 to just larger than you need for your project; add about 2.5cm (1in) all the way around if using scissors.

Whichever way you are cutting your project – lay the S133 onto your ironing surface that is covered with baking parchment, shiny side up. Lay a whole sheet or strips of decorated newspaper or leftover 'pretties' (whatever you have to hand) right side up onto the S133 until it is covered.

Lay a sheet of baking parchment over the whole project. Iron with a hot iron, moving the iron slowly over the surface for around 30 seconds. It is important to do this slowly as the heat has several layers to get through.

Wait for the project to cool right down – no peeking! Remove the baking parchment.

Your decorated S133 is now ready to cut to shape. If cutting smaller shapes for brooches, it is possible to cut the S133 with scissors. Once the shape has been cut then seal with at least 2 thin layers of acrylic wax. This milky coloured liquid dries clear and waterproof and gives a soft lustre to your work rather than a hard shine.

Once your decorated S133 is dry you can then assemble your project.

BELOW AND RIGHT A die-cutting machine can be useful when cutting shapes from the stiff, card-like S133. These shapes can also be cut using scissors or a craft knife – but take care!)

CHAPTER THREE

Working with Packaging

Working with packaging

Packaging materials are used every day by almost every company that manufactures and sells products. They protect against damage and adverse environmental conditions, make transportation easier, and make products attractive to the consumer. Although many companies are trying to adopt greener packaging alternatives, there is still plenty of packaging around that can find a second life in artistic creations.

Packaging can be made from many things; I have chosen to feature paper, card and food packaging in this book. It is very important only to work with products that are safe and will not give off any fumes when heated. Be wary of sharp edges on paper – paper cuts can be very painful. Never heat polystyrene, as the fumes are very dangerous. Limit yourself to stitching into it.

Paper and cardboard can be torn, layered, stitched, glued, curled, painted, printed, wrapped, stapled, decorated with painted Bondaweb – just as with any textile, except that they are not washable. After your next shopping trip, look at the packaging. Can you

paint it? Weave with it? Next time a parcel arrives, consider the potential of the wrappings. Whether you choose to work with shredded paper or chocolate wrappers, there is great fun to be had.

Isobel Moore

Isobel is inspired by colour, pattern and intricate detail. She likes to use natural fibres such as linen, cotton and handmade felt and can't help collecting pieces of brightly coloured silk, rainbow-dyed threads and tiny sparkling beads. Isobel is thrifty with her resources and often uses recycled fabrics and papers in her work, such as in the cardboard and wool basket below.

RIGHT This little basket, created by Isobel Moore at an evening workshop, is made from woven strips of cardboard packaging.

ABOVE Shaun West used partially shredded cardboard packaging as warp 'threads' to weave torn newspaper strips through. Once woven, the piece was decorated with print and hand stitch.

Shaun West

Shaun has a deep love of the beautiful south-west of England, where she lives, along with a keen interest in sustainability. Recycling and reuse have underpinned the rhythm of her life ever since she can remember. As well as making many textile items through the years, she has nurtured gardens out of wildernesses, filled them with reclaimed finds and grown green willow to make fences, dens, sculptures and baskets with found items woven in.

Shaun now has two young children and less time to spend on gardens and baskets. As the children grow, Shaun uses her snatches of free time to develop her love of producing decorative items from diverse materials. She thinks it is important to pass on to her children the lesson that recycling is a viable and imaginative alternative to throwing things away.

Shaun gets immense satisfaction from incorporating items that many would regard as rubbish into her work. She transforms these humble materials by combining them with paints, print, dye, glitter, fabrics and stitch to make something new and beautiful. In the piece on page 68, Shaun has used partially shredded cardboard packaging as the warp for weaving a weft of newspaper, recycled fabrics, threads, felt and plastics. The cardboard forms a good, strong support for the other materials and has a surface and texture that can be easily enhanced.

In the piece shown left, Shaun began by dyeing and then printing sheets of newspaper using a homemade block. Once the paper was dry, she tore it into regular strips, which she wove to create a new piece. To intergrate the layers and add further texture, she overprinted the surface and sewed into it using curving lines of straight stitches in a variety of threads. Notice how the stitching enhances the printed forms.

ABOVE Partially shredded cardboard packaging.
LEFT *Printed newspaper sample*. Newspaper torn into strips and woven together. If ironed onto a medium-weight iron-on interfacing such as Decovil 1, this piece would be strong enough to make a bag or a book cover.
OVERLEAF *Long sample*. Partially shredded cardboard packaging woven with packing tape, strips of paper and old fabrics.

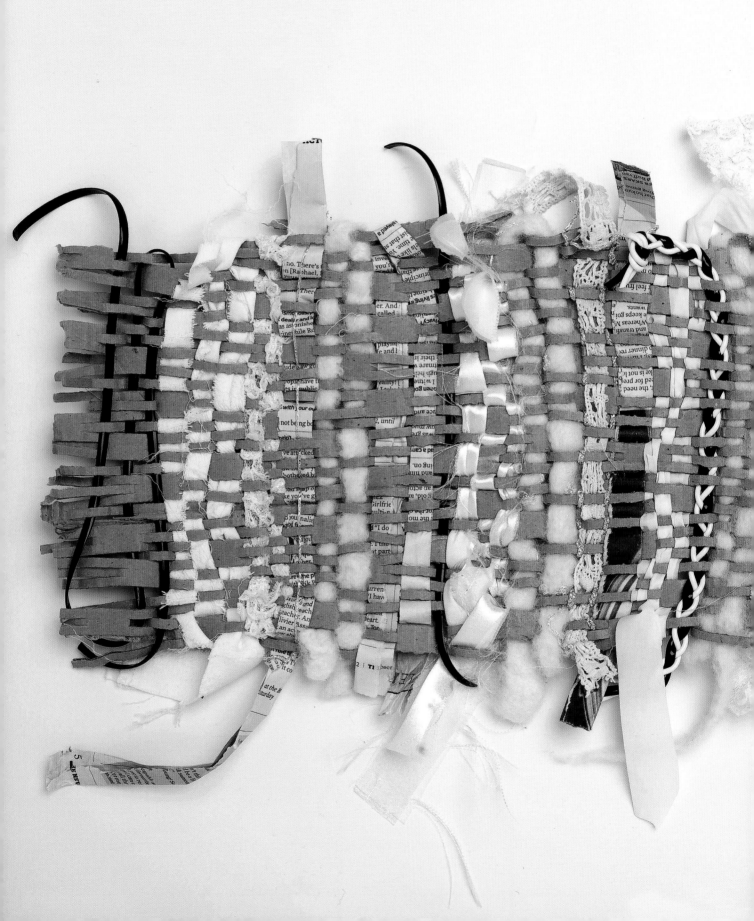

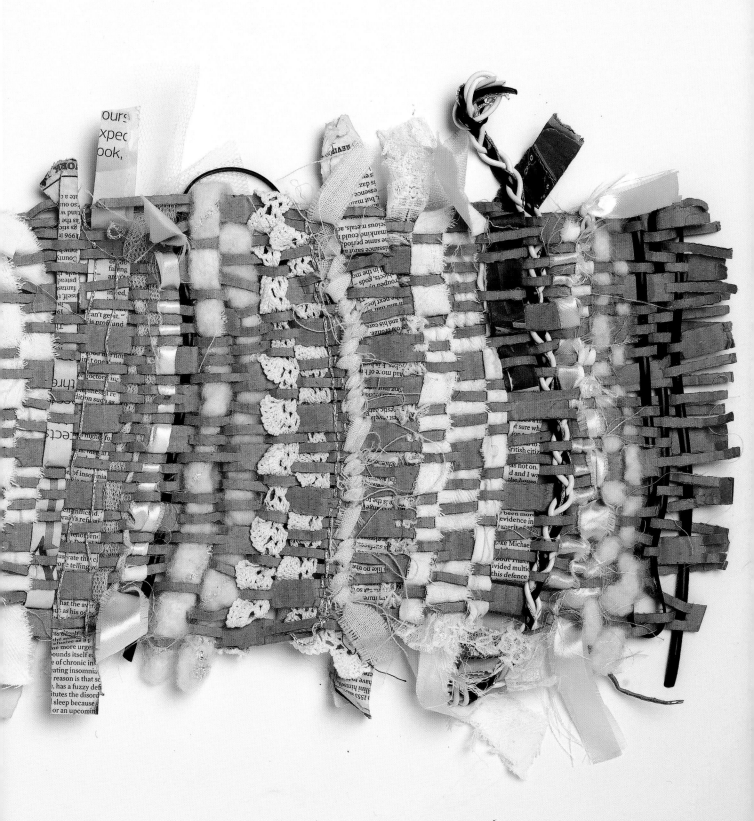

Shredded paper and painted Bondaweb sample

It says a lot about a person when she unpacks a parcel of long-awaited heat guns and is more excited about the packaging – shredded paper! There are many things you can do with strips of paper – weaving comes immediately to mind – but I fancied my usual fallback technique of layering with painted Bondaweb. After all my years of teaching and experimenting with the latest products, I still love Bondaweb the most. It is just so versatile. It can be ironed on to fabric, paper, wood and metal.

You will need
- Leftover scraps and strips of Bondaweb
- Water-based paints
- Strips of old magazines and/or newspaper
- Baking parchment
- An iron and stable ironing surface

Instructions

1 Paint the Bondaweb with a thin layer of water-based paint. Leave to dry.

2 Take ten strips of paper (whatever kind you have chosen) and lay them on a sheet of baking parchment, making sure the baking parchment is large enough for the size of your project. It is up to you how you arrange your papers – I tend to work in horizontal lines. Lay enough strips of painted Bondaweb onto the strips of paper to hold them and iron into place – don't forget to use the baking parchment between the iron and your work. Leave to cool completely.

3 Remove the backing paper from the Bondaweb and lay several more strips of paper on top. Iron into place. Again, don't forget to use the baking parchment between the iron and your work.

4 Repeat five times, until the sample is thick enough to handle and will not fall apart. Stitch into the sample with threads that tone with the painted Bondaweb. I used my usual random herringbone stitch in pink thread.

5 You could a create a fabulous little clutch bag by ironing this sample onto Decovil Light, a medium-weight interfacing with a leather-like feel, made by the manufacturers of Vilene. Protect the surface of the bag with several coats of acrylic wax.

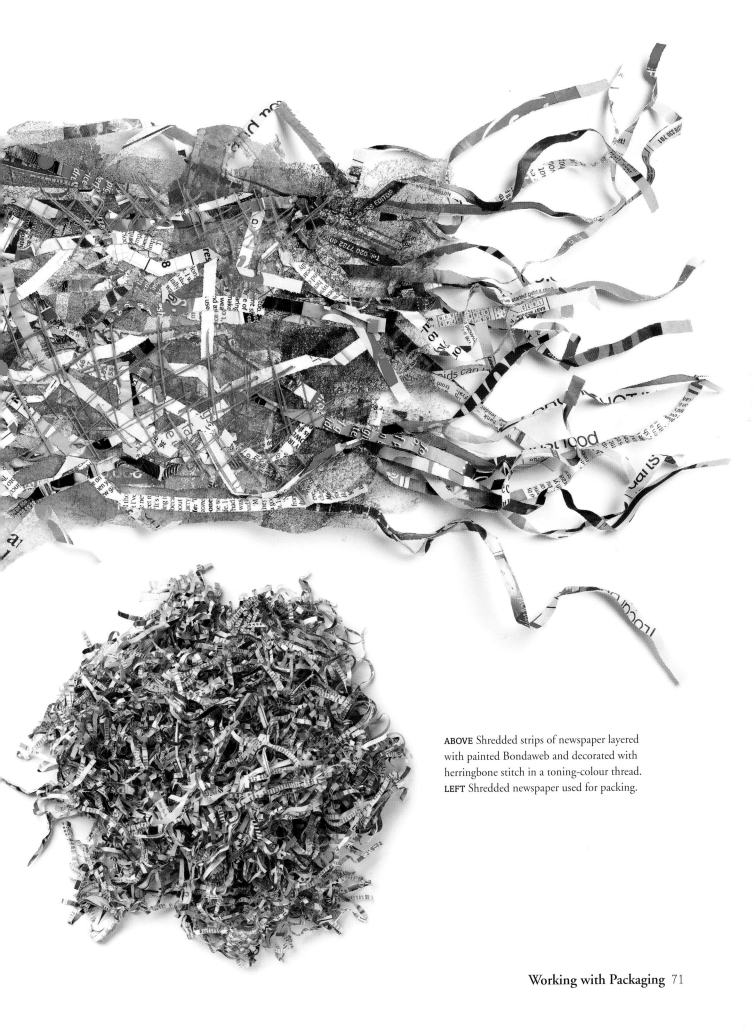

ABOVE Shredded strips of newspaper layered with painted Bondaweb and decorated with herringbone stitch in a toning-colour thread.
LEFT Shredded newspaper used for packing.

Kim Thittichai

Food packaging is great fun to work with, particularly chocolate wrappers and Magnum ice-cream wrappers – for obvious reasons, you have to eat the ice cream first… The shiny packaging comes in fabulous bright colours and can be distressed and made to pucker by ironing it lightly between pieces of baking parchment. The way to check whether a wrapper is the right type for texturing with an iron is to squeeze it in your hand: if it unfolds, it will work. If it has a 'memory' like tinfoil and stays in the shape that you have squeezed it into, it won't work. If you have ever distressed Tyvek with an iron, you will see that food packaging behaves in the same way.

One of the flower-shaped brooches is made from a Smarties wrapper (snack-sized) and the other is made from an almond Magnum ice-cream wrapper. The Smarties wrapper is very brightly coloured and the Magnum wrapper ranges from gold to bronze. Just gorgeous! I textured the wrappers with an iron and then ironed them on to very heavy iron-on pelmet Vilene, code number S133, to make the brooches strong enough to wear. I then cut the interfaced wrappers to shape using a die-cutting machine (the sort used by card-makers). All I had to do then was to glue a brooch pin on the back of the shapes.

ABOVE Brooches made from ironing chocolate wrappers (top) onto S133 heavy iron-on interfacing, and cutting them to shape with a die-cutting machine.
RIGHT Strips of chocolate wrappers pressed onto Solufix, covered in a layer of Solufleece and free machine stitched to hold all the strips in place.

Sweet-wrapper free machine sample

I created the lacy sample shown at the bottom of this page by collecting lots of chocolate wrappers and then cutting them into strips, which I pressed (by hand) on to a self-adhesive, water-soluble fabric called Solufix. (This product is very sticky to the touch and will also hold quite firm threads in place.) Another layer of Solufix went over the top before I stitched the whole piece with free machine embroidery in a random design. It is important, when using water-soluble products, to make sure that all your stitches link together, otherwise all the stitching will fall apart when you come to dissolve the product!

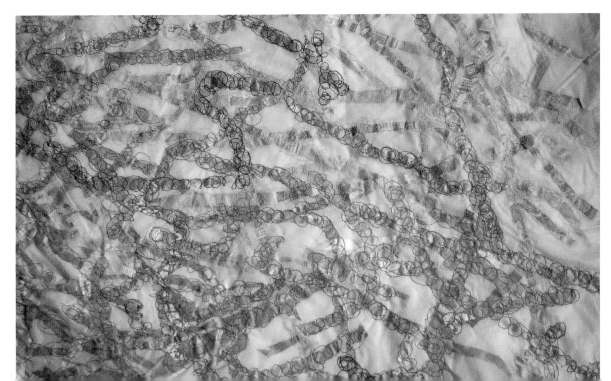

Claire Muir

Claire Muir very kindly created this stunning flower hairslide from a piece of heat-textured foil food packaging for me. Heat-textured foil food packaging stays soft to the touch after it has been heated, and so can be machine-embroidered to great effect. You can add thin strips of heat-treated food wrapping to your work if it needs a bit of sparkle but think carefully about how much 'bling' your work needs as large areas may be too distracting. Shiny food packaging can be glued to your work, but I think it always looks best if you stitch it on.

Claire created the flower by free-machining the heat-textured foil inside leaf-shaped frames made of covered wire. She added small glass beads in a toning colour, soft feathers and beads on wire as the flower was assembled. The flower can be worn as a hair adornment or a brooch.

For more information about Claire Muir, see page 92.

LEFT A beautiful corsage by Claire Muir. The piece was created using shiny food packaging and free machine embroidery on water-solouble fabric.

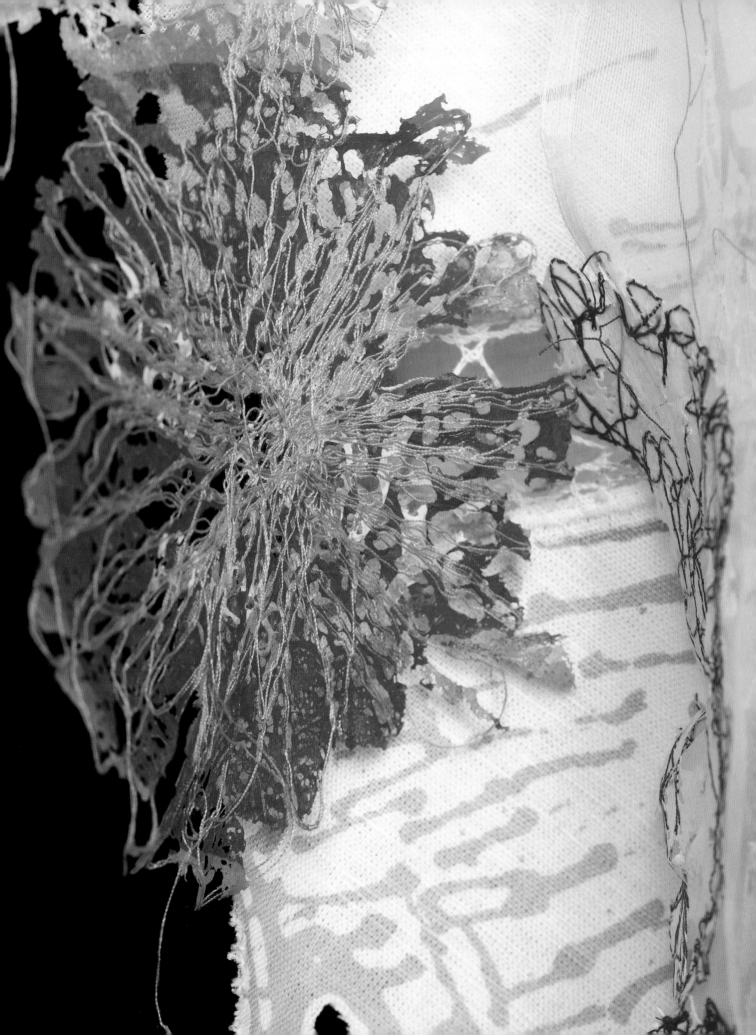

CHAPTER FOUR

Working with Plastic

Working with plastic

Since writing my first book, *Hot Textiles*, the way we dispose of plastics has changed quite dramatically. Much plastic packaging is now recyclable. For example, fleece garments can be created from recycled plastic bottles. Attitudes to our usage of plastics have changed too, and supermarkets' free plastic shopping bags may soon be a thing of the past.

There is a huge amount of information available on the Internet about how to recycle and the ways in which artists are using recycled materials. Plastic bags, bin liners and food packaging can be melted together by ironing them in between two sheets of non-stick baking parchment. The plastic will melt, soften and meld together. It is not necessary to apply great pressure when using this basic technique, as the heat does the work. It is possible to shape several layers of plastic whilst they are hot and they will keep the shape you have formed them into, but great care needs to be taken as molten plastic will stick to your skin and can remove the top layers. Wear suede gardening gloves while you are heating the plastic, quickly place the iron on a safe flat surface when you have finished, and shape the plastic while it is still hot. Hold it in shape while it cools.

When heating plastic, it is vital to work in a room with plenty of ventilation, or even outdoors. While it is very unlikely that the combination of plastics that you are melting will give off dangerous fumes, you can never be too careful.

There are several types of heat tool that you can use to melt, cut and shape plastic – a domestic iron, a heat press, a soldering iron and a heat gun. All will give a different effect.

• The iron and the heat press will melt the plastic into a flat piece. Baking parchment is needed underneath and on top of the plastic. Try cutting different coloured plastics into strips and melting them together.

• A soldering iron will cut through plastic, whether melted or not. The thicker the plastic, the more slowly you should move the soldering iron. Place your work on a smooth, heatproof surface such as a metal baking tray, toughened glass or a ceramic tile.

• A heat gun will melt plastic in a random fashion: wherever you apply the heat, the plastic will melt. It can be used to create fabulous melted edges on plastic vessels and bowls. Always work on a heatproof surface and be aware that hot plastic is really *hot*!

When sorting out plastics to work with, consider the colours that you are thinking of combining. Are they too contrasting? Would you prefer to work in tones of one colour? Just because you are experimenting doesn't mean that you should forget your colour sense.

Judith Hammond

Judith is a recent graduate in Design Crafts, who has produced an innovative contemporary lace from recycled plastic carrier bags. She wanted this common, throwaway item to be reused and admired, not discarded without thought. Approximately 13–17 billion plastic bags are used in the UK each year. On average we use over 200 plastic bags per person in the UK but recycle only one plastic bag in every 200 we use. The worldwide statistics are even more staggering. Globally we use between 500 billion and 1.2 trillion plastic bags per year, which averages out at over 1 million plastic bags used every minute.

Judith's current work has been inspired by traditional lace and two exhibitions. *Lost in Lace*, an exhibition featuring twenty leading international artists at Birmingham Museum and Art Gallery, drew attention to the qualities of lace, looking at the holes, spaces, structures and so on. The Crafts Council's touring exhibition *Block Party* showcased work by artists who have applied the aesthetics and techniques of pattern cutting to their practice in ways that were innovative and perhaps unexpected.

The influence of these two exhibitions can be seen in all four of the dresses featured here. In the past, lacemakers would tell stories while making lace; Judith's 'stories' – shopping lists, 'thoughts of the day' – and traditional lace motifs were transferred onto over 300 plastic carrier bags. She then heat-treated them to reveal a new,

LEFT *Multi-lace Dress*. A vintage linen tablecloth made into a dress and decorated with plastic carrier-bag 'lace'.
RIGHT *Orange Lace Boa Dress*. Vintage linen made into a dress and decorated with 'lace' made from plastic carrier bags. The 'lace' is suspended on fine nylon filament.

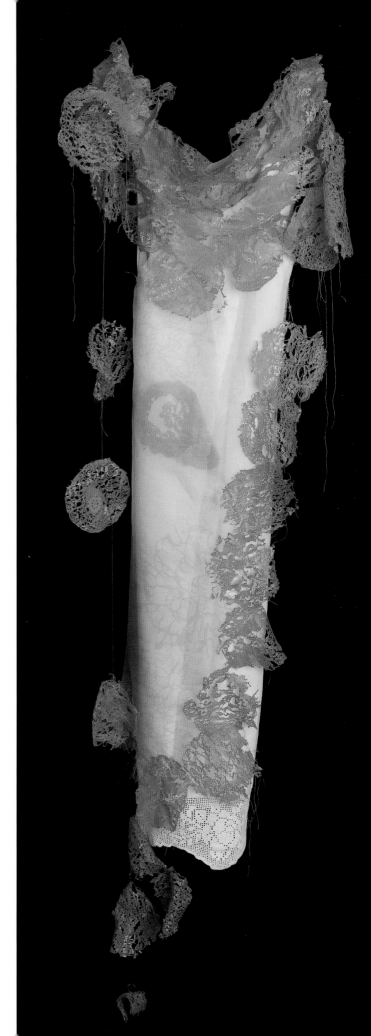

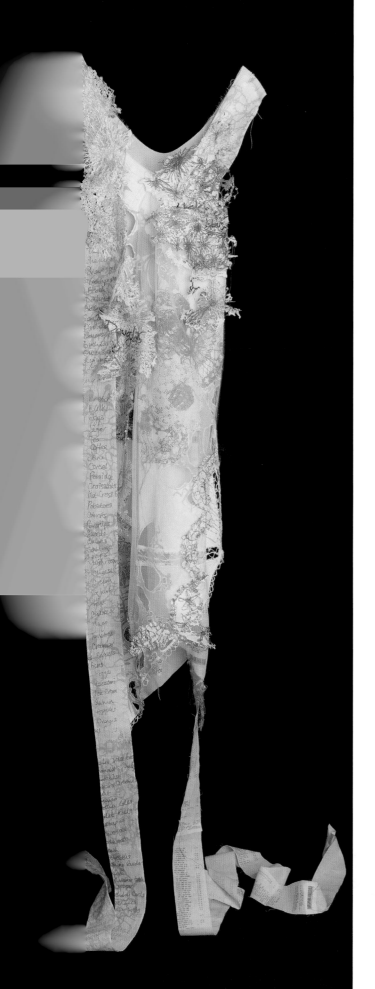

contemporary lace. The *Block Party* exhibition inspired the creation of Judith's layered dresses. Using found materials screen-printed with her own unique lace imagery and adorned with plastic carrier-bag lace, they are not intended to be worn but to exhibit creatively an innovative textile produced out of a non-traditional material. Judith's body of work demonstrates that plastic carrier-bag lace could be functional as a fashion adornment for new textiles or for upcycling garments; or it could be purely decorative, to be admired in its own right.

Since graduating, Judith has taken part in several exhibitions, worked as an artist in residence, and has been asked to give several lectures about her work. Her future plans are to continue to develop new textiles, whether for a particular exhibition or gallery, or purely for functional or for decorative purposes.

LEFT *Helen & Douglas House Dress* made from linen, print and 'lace' made from plastic carrier bags.
RIGHT *Orange Lace Dress.* This garment is made entirely from supermarket carrier bags.
PREVIOUS PAGE A detail from *Helen & Douglas House Dress.*

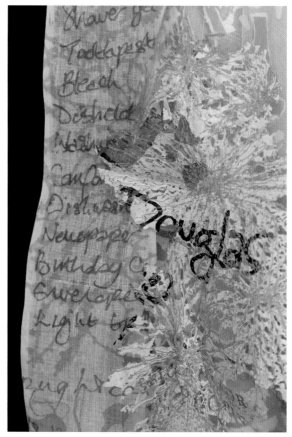

Mary Gray

I first met Mary when I was booked to deliver a lecture at her local Embroiderers' Guild. She told me about the project she had just finished for her City and Guilds course. It sounded right up my street as it involved the use of melted plastic carrier bags. When Mary sent me a photo of the finished work I was amazed, both at the size of the work and the workmanship. It is a wonderful piece of work.

Mary is fascinated by the dancing reflections on the surface of moving water – ever-changing, fragmented imagery that distorts reality. Whether the movement comes from the flow of a river, the rhythm of the sea or the wake of a swimmer in a pool, the effect is the same. The surface becomes multifaceted and fractured. There are areas of transparency, translucency and opacity, portraying different depths of water. Her work concerns the depiction of these strange, fractured reflections and transient moments of energy in cloth and stitch. She

finds that plastic, stitched and then heat-treated, creates the most fluid and water-like cloth. It bends, buckles, distorts, stretches, shrinks, fragments and produces different qualities of light.

The Swimmer

After making sketches of her daughter swimming in the local pool, Mary drew a larger image. The drawing was then simplified, with the different sections of colour clearly marked. Having sourced suitably coloured plastic carrier bags, Mary began to lay out the main design. It was a bit like piecing a jigsaw puzzle together. To achieve the effect of light and dark areas, she used darker or lighter coloured carrier bags underneath the main colour; the direction of the machine stitch and the use of shiny thread also helped.

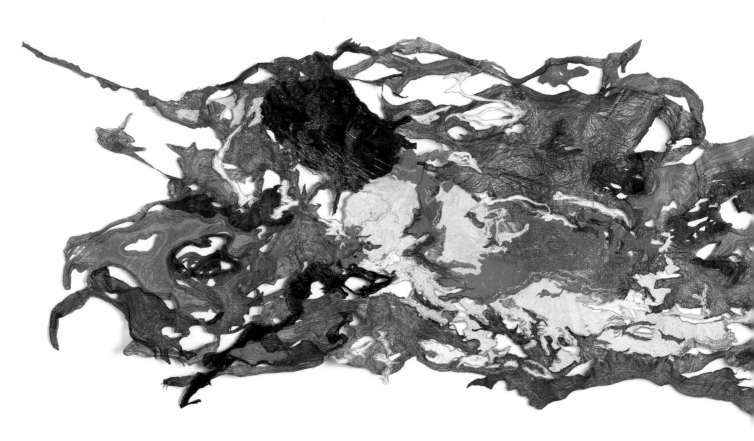

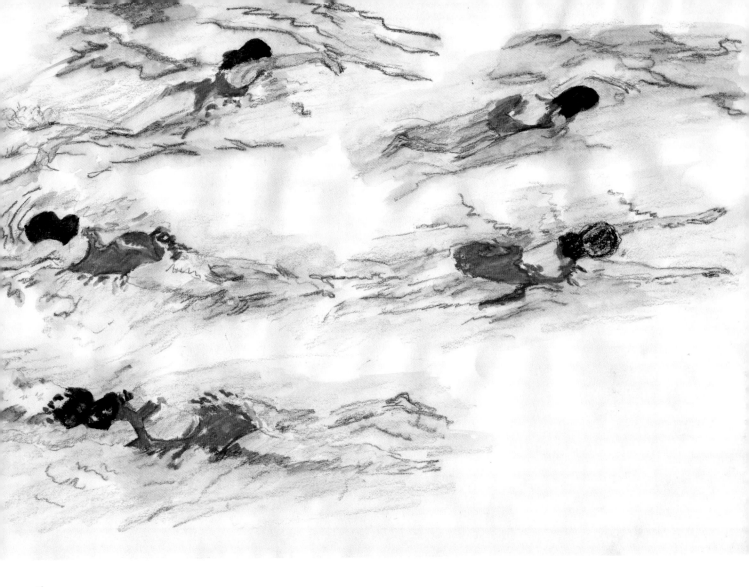

ABOVE Mary Gray's sketches of her daughter swimming. The sketches helped Mary to interpret the distortion of the water when making her work.

LEFT *The Swimmer* measures 30cm (12in) across. It is beautifully formed and finished and is a stunning interpretation of Mary's initial sketches.

Working with Plastic 85

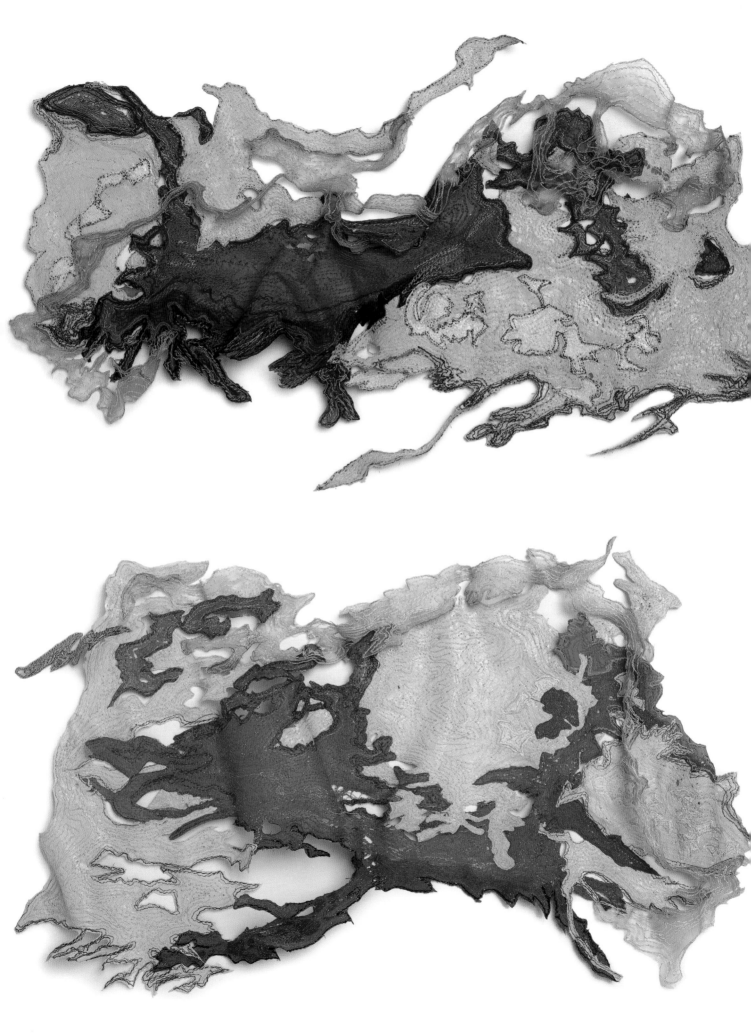

Mary stitched the plastic sections using free machine embroidery. She didn't want to use an embroidery ring as it would have stretched and damaged the thin plastic; a ring would also have got in the way of the large area that she needed to stitch in one go. The sections were stitched in concentric circles, starting at the widest point and getting smaller. She took care to keep the plastic taut and flat while she was stitching. The finished stitched sections were then ironed between pieces of baking parchment to melt the plastic. The use of different pressures and different lengths of time created some fabulous effects, from shrinkage to shine. Because there were holes in some of the sections, they distorted when ironed, which meant that the final stitching of the sections became quite a challenge. As with most problems when working with unusual materials, the unpredictability of the final joining of the sections created an undulating effect that actually helped to create the shimmering effect of the water.

LEFT A pair of working samples by Mary Gray. Sections of Mary's sketches (see page 85) developed into finished pieces that were mounted onto canvases.

ABOVE A working sample showing how the melted plastic creates marvellously distorted shapes when stitched together.

RIGHT Pencil case with zip
opening made from melted
plastic bags.

Laura Manning

Laura originally trained as a jeweller and studied in South Korea as part of her degree. She has always been interested in creative reuse but it was in South Korea that her passion developed when she began to experiment with found objects and 'rubbish'.

Laura likes to combine 'precious' materials with repurposed items to show that they have value too. Laura loves working with tatty old knitting needles, fabric, plastic bags, milk bottles and other plastics. It

means a lot to her to show the hidden beauty of the detritus from our everyday lives. She also uses antique and vintage buttons, in conjunction with silver or Eco Gold (recycled gold), to make unique items.

The pencil case above was created by melting several layers of plastic carrier bags between baking parchment to form a 'fabric' that could be cut and stitched to make new items. Garments such as the earrings and masks shown here are made from discarded household plastics.

LEFT These lovely flower-shaped stud earrings were cut from a plastic milk carton.
RIGHT Masks made from netting, string and various plastics.

ABOVE AND RIGHT Masks made by Laura Manning and the students in the Craft Design Technology class she teaches.

Laura and her students have layered fabrics, such as net, satin fabric, ribbon and string, in between layers of plastic carrier bags and bubble wrap. These layers have been ironed between sheets of baking parchment and then left to cool. The resulting layers are quite firm and can be cut with scissors to create hole for the eyes. The layers would still be soft enough to bend around your face to create a mask. When melting plastics always work in a very well-ventilated room or outside. For more information on melting plastics, see page 12.

Claire Muir

Claire Muir specializes in making machine-embroidered flowers, incorporating whatever is needed to make the flowers stand out, including melted plastics. Claire received a first-class honours degree in Art and Related Arts from Bishop Otter College, Chichester, West Sussex, and followed it with a year's postgraduate study in the Textiles Department of Glasgow School of Art. Her subsequent employment as a designer of headdresses and accessories for Stageworks Worldwide Productions enabled her to experiment with a wide range of techniques and materials. She has since developed this knowledge further, as displayed in her current creations.

Claire creates exquisite flowers, fascinators and all manner of tiaras and one-off pieces of jewellery. Her flowers are very well observed, due to the time she takes in the study of plant forms. She chooses flowers with an open appearance such as lilies, hibiscus, clematis and open roses. Flowers that grow in tight forms are not suitable for Claire's embroidered lace technique.

Anyone who has a Claire Muir fascinator or flower in her possession will know about the 'boing' factor that Claire is so passionate about. She only uses a certain type of wire, which is firm enough to support the different elements that she uses to embellish her work, but also has a 'bouncy' quality to ensure that the whole flower or added embellishment trembles when the wearer moves her head. My orange flower fascinator, made from a melted carrier bag, has extra-small machine-embroidered 'leaves' that 'boing' about when it is worn. The gentle bounce that the separate elements have makes the fascinator a moving work of art.

Claire regularly exhibits her work and demonstrates her skills at exhibitions countrywide. She delivers lectures and workshops nationally and also runs practical workshops in her studio in Birmingham.

RIGHT A wonderful hair adornment by Claire Muir. The piece was made using a melted plastic carrier bag and free machine embroidery, and embellished with feathers, wire and crystal beads.

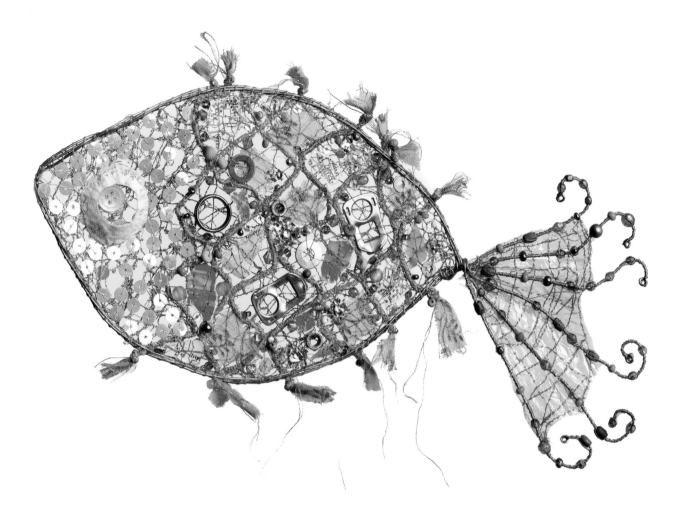

Isobel Moore

The work of machine-embroidery teacher Isobel Moore shows that beauty can be found in many unexpected items, and that no matter how small, such objects can be put to good use. Isobel has always been a maker. Growing up, she learned to knit and crochet, but it was when she was allowed to play with a sewing machine that her passion for stitched textiles began. For many years she made small stitched gifts and cards based on ideas gleaned from books. Then she discovered the world of machine embroidery and has never looked back! Having completed her City and Guilds Diploma in Machine Embroidery, she now teaches machine embroidery and exhibits her own work. She has a particular interest in creating three-dimensional work.

Flotsam and Jetsam

Two fish, Flotsam and Jetsam, formed Isobel's winning entry in a competition of the same name run by her local Embroiderers' Guild. The topic was close to her heart: she has always been inspired by the sea and is also a bit of an eco-warrior, regularly using recycled linens, cottons, silks, rainbow-dyed threads, papers and sparkling beads in her work. Isobel's students have been known to tease her as she never lets them throw anything away, even collecting all their scraps at the end of a lesson – so finding enough 'flotsam and jetsam' to create these pieces was never going to be a problem!

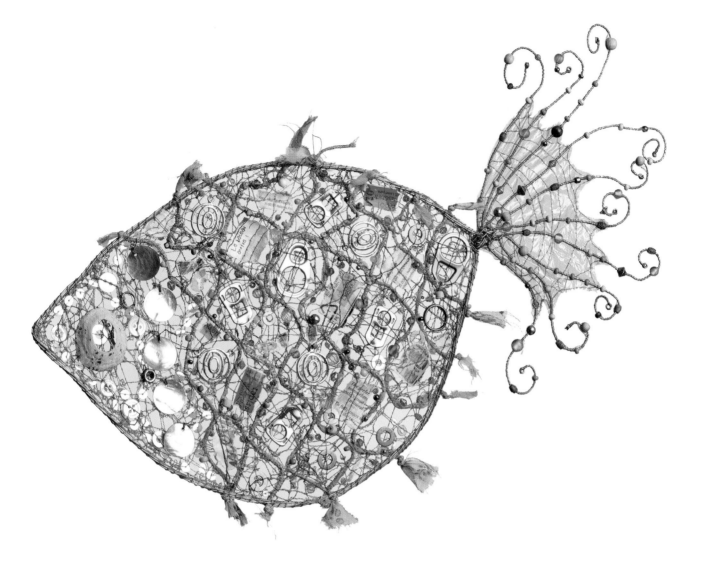

To make the fish, Isobel machine-wrapped ripped recycled fabrics to create beaded cords, then, using second-hand threads, stitched these to a base of water-soluble fabric to form a background mesh. She threaded the ends of the cords through the twists of an armature made from copper earth wire, holding them in place with knots and more beads. For the tails of the fish, Isobel used fused plastic freezer bags. Finally, she used machine stitching to attach assorted recycled sequins, washers, ring-pulls and papers. The eyes were made from shells collected on a summer holiday in Brittany, France.

ABOVE *Flotsam and Jetsam* by Isobel Moore.

CHAPTER FIVE

Working with Mixed Media

Working with mixed media

Many artists enjoy employing more than one medium in their work, and the term 'mixed media' can cover a multitude of media, both wet and dry. With recycling becoming more popular, so the products we use in our work are changing. Even new technology is playing a part. Products such as gel mediums, which are made to extend the working time of acrylic paint, have become very popular in recent years, used instead as an archival-quality glue, or slightly watered down as a varnish. Another useful product for sealing your work is acrylic wax. With many of us choosing to mount our work on canvas, these mediums have become invaluable.

I hope that the work in this chapter will demonstrate the versatility of different media. As well as stitch, it covers fabric, paper, paint, thread, pages recycled from books, and drawings.

Cas Holmes and Anne Kelly

Cas Holmes has long been known as the eco-warrior of the textiles world, and I have always admired her work and the ethos behind it. Her work relates to the natural and built world and draws attention to the places and things around us we sometimes overlook. Cas exhibits and delivers lectures and workshops internationally. She is the author of *The Found Object in Textile Art*.
Anne Kelly works with vintage fabrics sourced from jumble sales and charity shops. Using old tablecloths, samplers, and stitched and printed canvas, she creates exciting, textured and heavily stitched hangings and pictures. Anne is particularly interested in the everyday aspect of vintage textiles and uses them to create a new and seamless fabric.

Both Cas and Anne draw regularly, and this adds a greater depth to their work as the pictorial parts of it are well observed. They began to collaborate five years ago, after seeing each other's work at a local exhibition. Since then, they have exhibited jointly, producing site-specific pieces for each venue. In both individual and joint works they use a range of recycled, upcycled and found materials and fabric. These are altered using a number of fine-art techniques, including drawing and painting,

but their expression of line is clearly distinct. Cas and Anne exhibit regularly and together have written *Connected Cloth – Creating Collaborative Textile Projects*.

Garden Paths

Cas and Anne's collaborative work *Garden Paths* arose from their interest in domestic spaces and the surrounding environment. Cas's focus for this piece was determined by her broken arm and having to concentrate on her immediate surroundings – things seen along the path itself. Anne's work reflects the views from her garden and shed (which acts as a gallery during the month of June and where *Garden Paths* was also exhibited). This work has been shown in a library, another shed, a hospital and a theatre gallery since then.

Starting points were taken from an agreed size and subject matter, and as always began with some common materials. Cas and Anne used journals and garden sketchbooks to inform the content of the pieces. When they met up to discuss how the project was progressing, they were surprised to discover that they were working

to different-sized formats. However, they felt that the work benefited from this and reflected the irregularity of a garden path and their individual approaches. Cas's pieces observe small changes along the pathway over a three-month period and include a sketch of a dead magpie (drawn with her left hand). This intimate approach relies on combining painterly marks with dye and printed, stitched and overlaid fabrics, some printed directly from plant materials, and incorporating fabric that had been buried at the edges of the path (Cas buries fabric so that it becomes marked by the earth and by time).

Anne's pieces combine photographic and printed images on vintage fabric. The book image at the top of each panel was taken from her collection of antique natural-history books. She added stitched drawings of plants from her garden and appliquéd flowers constructed from old sheeting, using reclaimed buttons to attach them to the backing.

LEFT Part One of *Garden Paths* by Cas Holmes.

LEFT Part Two of *Garden Paths* by Cas Holmes.

RIGHT Anne Kelly's interpretation of the work *Garden Paths*.

certain plants in
each group demand
special treatment

bench

hellebore

the garden

students are available

charleston head tiles

verbena

the shed

Stephanie Redfern

After twenty years as a ceramicist, Steph began to concentrate upon textiles and mixed media. She uses paint, print and dye on most of her fabrics, enjoying the immediate sensation of colour and mark-making, and goes on to incorporate collage and stitching. Her inspirations are the suburban landscape, the wider landscape, architecture, pattern, and all aspects of the natural world. Steph uses a wide variety of materials as well as fabric and paper, which she paints and prints using acrylic paints and inks, according to the project. These include natural products such as bark, quirky found objects, ceramic pieces and waste materials such as tomato paste tubes. The transformation of the everyday into subtle and at times esoteric symbolism is frequently a presence in her work.

Steph makes design sheets and drawings before starting to work on a project, but the work also evolves from, and is dictated by, the source materials. She collects together cloth, threads and found objects and then organizes and layers the design. All the elements are then machine- and hand-stitched together to produce the finished work. This method is usually, but not always, controllable. Steph comments: 'Quirky, wonderful surprises can happen due to the juxtaposition of the shapes and colours of the appliqué. Many of the best things that happen are unplanned, but strangely still represent that inexplicable end result that is a combination of personality, experience, life and the patterns and spaces that surround me.'

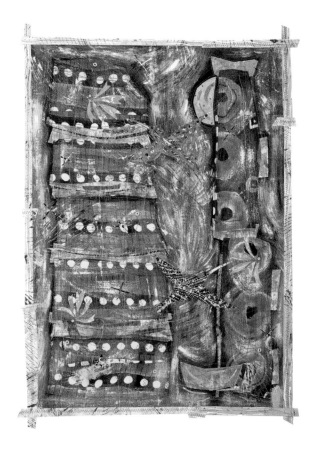

Steph also uses her own writing in her work, more so since she has started to make artist's books. Two years ago, she started work on an ongoing project she has entitled 'Thrift and Alchemy', a series of pieces of work including an artist's book called *White Noise*. The materials in these works, including the pieces shown here, are all recycled: nothing is new except the paint and some of the threads and beads. Her latest aim is to use mixed-media materials in a such a way that it is not immediately obvious what a piece of work is made from, and to include unusual objects or materials that reveal themselves upon close examination of the work. Steph has won several prizes for her textile work, exhibits frequently and her work has been featured in several publications. She has also self-published her artist's books – *Cacao Grove* in 2009 and *The Stone Bird* in 2011.

LEFT *Floating*. Paper, fabric, emulsion paint and machine stitch.
ABOVE *Hummingbirds*. Paper, fabric, gesso and machine stitch.
RIGHT *Rainforest*. Paper, fabric, gesso and machine stitch.

Kim Thittichai

This collection of work was started at a summer school and eventually finished at home. The tutor was Jan Evans, who introduced the group to natural pigments or ochres that are mined in the Clearwell Caves in the Forest of Dean, close to where she lives. We were encouraged to use only the colours of the ochres – yellow, brown, red and purple. As the ochres were in powder form, we mixed them with gel mediums to make them easier to use, like a paint.

We made textured blocks from drawings produced on the course and then made rubbings from the blocks on various papers, using graphite sticks to make the marks. These rubbings were then layered with papers, scrim and photocopied sections of our drawings. The layered pieces were then stitched and finally stuck to ochre-coloured canvases.

LEFT AND ABOVE *Earth Traces One and Two*. Tracing paper decorated with graphite, layered over hemp fibres on handmade paper.
RIGHT *Earth Traces Three*. Photocopied designs were stitched onto layers of scrim and painted Bondaweb.

Mary Moox

If you are ever wondering what to do with that beautifully shaped stone you found on the beach, or the gorgeous scrap of fabric you cannot part with, take a look at the work of Mary Moox. Mary first came to my attention when she joined my Experimental Textiles course ten years ago. Her use of recycled materials fascinated me at time when recycling was still quite unusual. Her work is very popular and held in many private collections all over the world. Her creations are born of an inherited addiction to 'Womble-ing': her dad's description for walking the dogs and returning with half a bicycle and an armful of old wood, much to her mother's dismay. Mary likes to collect rejected textile 'stuff', nicely shaped stones and shells, and make them into little characters. It fascinates her to see how she can create naughty, haughty, shy or flamboyant little creatures out of inanimate junk. Some are endearing, some a little macabre, but that is part of their charm. Nothing is safe from Mary – even old boxes, drawers and crates become homes for her special creatures.

ABOVE One of Mary Moox's delightful creatures, created using all manner of reclaimed materials.

Judy Martin

Judy Martin is a painter and teacher. She studied painting and printmaking at Maidstone College of Art and went on to complete a postgraduate degree at Reading University. Judy was a freelance writer and editor for fifteen years and is the author of several practical art books. She has worked in adult education and a mental health centre, facilitating groups in art, craft and ceramics.

Her work runs in series, sometimes exploring the potential of a single image from a newspaper or magazine; sometimes delving into a broad subject such as movement or dance, or the form of the local landscape. In recent years, her work has primarily been concerned with figure and portrait subjects drawn from a variety of sources.

The images are allowed to evolve in ways that may take them beyond the original subject, resulting in a combination of observed and invented elements. Surface qualities are important: each picture is uniquely formed by the material and processes used. I find her use of fabric, old tights, pillowcases and paint quite fascinating: it is always interesting to discover how artists formulate ideas.

Dancing Dolls

Although Judy is ostensibly a fine artist working with paint, she is also a great creator of collage. *Dancing Dolls* grew from an idea she had after making a series of drawings of people standing or sitting in rows. Judy combined this idea with another thread that had been lurking at the back of her mind – mummification and body wrapping. After seeing an exhibition of work by the German artist Thomas Schutte, for which the artist had made life-size wrapped sculptures, Judy's ideas began to formulate. Her wrapped dolls are 15cm (6in) tall. Judy is very careful when choosing fabrics for her projects. Not just type of print and colour combinations, but how the material will drape.

Once she had finished the dolls, Judy made a series of drawings and watercolours and then started on the larger painting/collage shown above I love the sense of movement she has achieved.

LEFT Dolls made by wrapping fabric around ice-lolly sticks and wrapping again with thread so that the doll held in place.
ABOVE A collage showing all the dancing dolls.

Book slip cover

This book slip cover was made with a medium-weight iron-on interfacing called Decovil 1 from Freudenberg Vilene which is soft and leathery to the touch and makes fabulous slip covers for books; it is also ideal for making belts and bags.

You will need
• **Book to cover**
• **Decovil 1 iron-on interfacing – enough to wrap around your book plus 10cm (4in)**
• **Acrylic paints**
• **Newspaper decorated with painted Bondaweb and gilding flakes (or leftover 'pretties', see page 51), torn into strips**
• **Roll of baking parchment**
• **Acrylic wax**
• **Sewing machine**

ABOVE A decorative book slip cover made using Decovil 1 iron-on interfacing.

Instructions

1 To measure the width of the book: take a tape measure and, starting 5cm (2in) inside the front cover, close the book, continue measuring around the book, around the spine, across the back cover of the book, then open the back cover and measure another 5cm (2in) inside. This measurement will be the width you need to cut for your slip cover. For the depth of the book just add 0.6cm (¼in) to the depth of the book. You just need enough room to stitch a narrow seam top and bottom of the cover and have enough 'give' to slip the covers of the book into the slip cover. If in doubt, you could make a pattern from newspaper before you cut the interfacing.

2 Cut the interfacing to size and then paint it on both sides with watered-down acrylic paint, in the proportions of two-thirds water to one-third paint. (If you paint the adhesive side of the interfacing with paint that is too thick, you will stop the glue from being activated when heat is applied.) Cover all the interfacing.

3 When the interfacing is dry, lay strips of decorated newspaper on the adhesive side (shiny side) and iron them on using baking parchment underneath and on top of your work.

4 Coat the book cover with acrylic wax to protect the surface. Fold over the ends of the piece to create flaps for the book to slip into and machine-stitch close to the edge.

Lamifix purse

This little pocket was made in a similar way to the book cover, but I
used Decovil 1Light, which is about half the weight of Decovil 1 and
yet still has a leathery feel. It is fabulous for many craft projects.

To seal the work, I ironed gloss Lamifix on to it. Lamifix is an iron-on
plastic laminate, available in matt or gloss, which you can use to make
work waterproof. It is very handy for bags and books. Lamifix can be
bought by the metre and you iron it on using baking parchment.

The work was then cut to shape with a die-cutting machine but this
thickness of interfacing is easy to cut with scissors, so you could cut
around a template to make the shape.

Bangles

Like many of you, I am a collector. Of fabric, tools, sewing machines, threads, all manner of packaging and plastic – and of course books. We can't have enough books. Of course it does help if you read them! I also collect old jewellery and beads for that wonderful day when I no longer have to work and can start to create some kind of amazing sculptural project. In the meantime, I have used some of my bead hoard to make these bangles. They employ fencing wire for the base of the bangle and a finer wire with a 'memory' to string the smaller beads (a wire with memory holds the shape it is twisted into).

You will need

For the main bangle:
• **Large beads sorted into colour (making sure the holes are big enough to fit the fencing wire)**
• **Fencing wire**
For the decoration:
• **Smaller glass beads in a colour toning with the bangle beads**
• **Finer wire**

Instructions

1 Cut the fencing wire to the size required to go around your wrist, but making it loose enough to get your hand through, adding an extra 5cm (2in) for wrapping the ends together.

2 Thread the large beads on to this wire (they have a hole big enough for the wire to go through). Leave 5cm (2in) of wire without beads.

3 Take one end of the wire and make a loop with it. Thread the other end through the loop before forming it into another loop. Make sure the loops hold the bangle together.

4 Take the fine wire and cut it to a length three times the length of the fencing wire. Thread it with small glass beads, leaving 2.5cm (1in) free at each end. Finish off by threading the wire back through the last few glass beads and wrap any excess around the gap between beads.

5 Take the fine wire threaded with glass beads and start to wrap it around the large bangle. I tend to start to wrap and then go back on myself to secure the first end.

6 Carry on wrapping around the bangle. It's up to you whether you make the wraps close together with little space in between, and go around the bangle only once, or whether you make the wraps further apart and go around the bangle two or three times. Once you have finished, wiggle the end of the fine wire into the space between two of the large beads and wrap it around the fencing wire.

7 Wrapping the fine beaded wire around the thick beaded wire helps the bangle merge into a single entity by filling in gaps and making the whole thing more secure. As to choice of colour – it's up to you.

Wooden box

I paint a lot of Bondaweb for use at shows and workshops; I like to have a good selection on hand. There are always odd little bits left over from projects or demonstrations that I can't throw away – does that sound familiar?

Bondaweb can be ironed on to anything flat that will take heat: paper, card, wood, metal and, of course, fabric. Here I've used a cheap box made from balsa wood, which I colourwashed blue with Procion dye powder and water. When the box was dry I ironed pink and gold Bondaweb directly on to the box.

You will need
- Small balsa wood box
- Procion dye powder, colour to suit
- Scraps of Bondaweb to paint (or you could use some you have already painted)
- Water-based paints
- Roll of baking parchment
- Gilding flakes
- Acrylic wax
- Iron and stable ironing surface

Instructions

1 Make up the colourwash solution using 1 teaspoonful of dye powder to 500ml (1 pint) water. Brush it over the box and leave it to dry.

2 Paint the rough side of the Bondaweb with watered-down paint and leave it to dry. Tear it into ragged strips, then iron these on to the box, remembering to use baking parchment between the layers to protect the iron.

3 Allow the Bondaweb to cool, then sprinkle it with gilding flakes. Gilding flakes need careful handling, as they can blow away if you breathe too hard. When you sprinkle them on, use sparingly, and gently rub them into place before you iron them onto the painted Bondaweb. Use baking parchent to protect your iron. Leave to cool.

4 When you are happy with the decoration, seal the box with three coats of acrylic wax.

Little Fishes in the Deep canvas

Followers of my blog will know of my continuing love affair with dyed and painted newspaper. I use newspaper to protect my table when dyeing and painting products. Because I use metallic paints, the papers build up wonderful layers of colour as I dry them out and use them over and over again. I can no longer throw them away!

This *Little Fishes* project uses such newspapers with printed and painted Bondaweb, and a printing block to make the fish. However, you could choose a different subject or just play with pattern. It is a very 'loose' process. Once you have prepared, printed and stitched all the materials you need, you can begin to compose the finished canvas. You don't have to use stitch in this project, but it can add texture to the surface. If you don't wish to use a sewing machine, you can always embellish your newspaper prints with hand stitch. If you enjoy doing water-soluble embroidery, you could add free-machine-stitched shapes of your choice and iron them on to your printed and painted Bondaweb. I've also used Jones Tones foils. These are the best foils I have found and they work every time.

You will need
- **A box canvas**
- **Newpaper with paint and dye applied (see page 50)**
- **Paste (wallpaper paste is fine)**
- **Soft paintbrush, 5cm (2in) wide**
- **Vilene Stitch 'n' Tear: 30cm x 60cm (12 x 24in)**
- **1 x A4 sheet of medium Hot Spots**
- **Jones Tones transfer foil**
- **Bondaweb (enough to cover the canvas and also to back the newspaper)**
- **1 or 2 printing blocks, depending on your subject. You could use commercial wooden or rubber blocks, or your own homemade kind.**
- **Paint thick enough to print with (I use Colourful Thoughts' multi-surface paints because they are *so* metallic)**
- **Dimensional resist paste**
- **Sponge to apply paint to the printing block**
- **Roll of baking parchment**
- **Varnish or acrylic wax**
- **Iron and ironing board**
- **Sewing machine (optional)**

Instructions

1 Mix the paste and, using the paintbrush, paste torn strips of the painted newspaper and stick them to the canvas. Leave to dry overnight.

2 Use the paintbrush to paint the Bondaweb for the canvas on the rough side (this is the sticky side; the smooth side is the backing paper, which you will remove later). You want a soft merging of colours, not stripes. Leave to dry overnight.

When painting Bondaweb, you need to make sure that the paint is thin enough to see through. If the paint is too thick, the Bondaweb won't stick to its intended surface. Particular care needs to be taken when using latex-based paints – they are worth using because of their high metallic content, but can form a barrier and stop Bondaweb from sticking, so make sure you water them down by at least half. As you paint the Bondaweb, the backing paper will ripple, creating a lovely textured effect.

BELOW The finshed *Little Fishes* artwork.

ABOVE Paints, printing blocks, dimensional resist, Bondaweb, Stitch 'n' Tear.

1

2

3a

3b

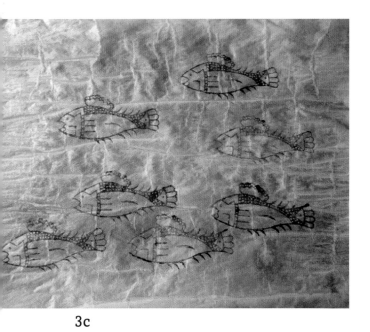

3c

3d

4

5a

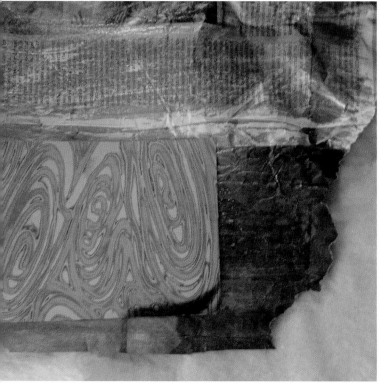
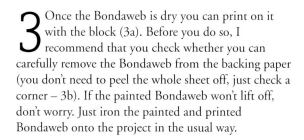

5b

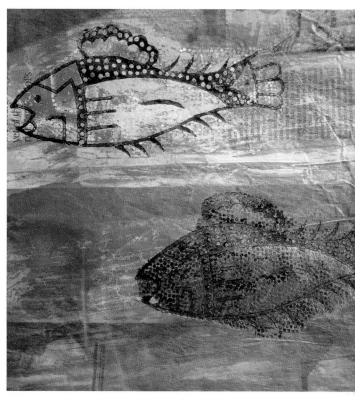

5c

3 Once the Bondaweb is dry you can print on it with the block (3a). Before you do so, I recommend that you check whether you can carefully remove the Bondaweb from the backing paper (you don't need to peel the whole sheet off, just check a corner – 3b). If the painted Bondaweb won't lift off, don't worry. Just iron the painted and printed Bondaweb onto the project in the usual way.

When printing with wooden or rubber blocks, I use a car sponge cut into wedges to apply the paint to the block rather than a roller or brayer (3d). You can choose whichever is best for you. Don't flood the block with paint or you will lose the definition of the print. If you are using a new block, do a few trial prints to check the amount of paint you need. As you are going to tear up the prints, it doesn't really matter if they are a bit hit and miss. I use paper plates as a palette, which I save to tear up and stitch into.

4 Now print on some of the painted newspaper. I like to choose sections of newspaper that have a combination of random splodges of metallic paint and dye. This is an almost accidental way of working.

You never quite know how your project will look until you have finished.

5 For extra sparkle, take the sheet of Hot Spots and draw around the printing block on the back of it. Cut out the shape with paper scissors. With a hot iron, iron the shape (spot-side down) on to the newspaper, using baking parchment to protect the iron (5a). Leave to cool, then remove the baking parchment and the Hot Spots brown backing paper. The clear spots will be revealed, and can then be foiled. Lay the foil colour-side up on the spots of glue (5b). Cover with baking parchment and iron with a warm iron for three seconds. Leave to cool and then peel off the foil to reveal your shiny fish shape (5c). This can then be printed on and stitched into.

6 An optional step. Once the print on the newspaper is dry, back it with Stitch 'n' Tear interfacing and free-machine around and into the print. It really is up to you just how much you embellish your print. Once you have finished stitching, carefully remove the interfacing, taking care not to tear the newspaper in the wrong place.

6

7

7 Cut plain, unpainted Bondaweb to back the sheets of printed (and optionally stitched) newspaper. Make sure that there is no Bondaweb sticking out around the edges, as this will contaminate the baking parchment and transfer to your work where you don't want it. Lay baking parchment on the ironing board. Place the printed newspaper print-side down on top. Lay the pre-cut plain Bondaweb rough-side down on the back of the newspaper. Cover everything with another layer of baking parchment and iron with a hot iron for 10–30 seconds or so, depending on the size of the piece you are working on. Leave to cool.

8 You can now start to lay out torn sections on the canvas and decide on a pleasing composition. Tear sections of the printed and painted Bondaweb, take them off the backing paper and lay them on the canvas.

8

9 Tear off sections of printed newspaper to add to the composition. Do not iron anything in place yet! (When you come to iron in place, make sure you remove the backing paper from the Bondaweb beforehand.)

10 Lay your chosen printed newspaper sections on the canvas. Play around with the composition, overlapping Bondaweb and papers in whichever order you wish. It is your composition: enjoy making those small decisions.

11 Once you are sure of the composition, carefully cover the entire surface of the canvas with baking parchment and iron everything in place. Leave to cool before you peel off the baking parchment.

12 You can further embellish the canvas with dimensional resist paste. This paste is thick enough to use with stencils and printing blocks and dries clear. It can be mixed with various mica powders and paints to great effect. I wanted to finish the canvas with an impression of curly waves, to make it look as though my little fishes were swimming in the sea. I used a pearlescent tinting medium mixed with the resist paste for an almost see-through effect. Once you have finished decorating the canvas, protect it with a non-yellowing varnish or acrylic wax.

Conclusion

So… it's time to play! Will you start to look at the contents of your recycling box as a treasure trove? There are not many materials that cannot be reused in some way. They can be cut, coloured, glued or stitched. Some can even be melted, but take care and if you are not sure whether a material will give off fumes when you melt it, and instead be happy with melting chocolate and ice-cream wrappers. Crisp packets work well too. Always carry out melting exercises in a well-ventilated area.

It has never been easier to view other people's work. With access to the Internet, the whole world is your oyster, but don't forget to get out into the world to see exhibitions and galleries. There is no substitute for viewing artists' work in real life, seeing at first hand how the work is hung, the textures of it and, of course, the colour. Is the work viewed by looking down on it or up at it? Everything makes a difference. Colours will always change when photographed and seeing work second- or third-hand on a computer screen cannot compete with this. I appreciate that it is not always possible for everyone to visit many exhibitions a year – but do try.

Copyright

There is a danger that with the ease of viewing someone else's work on your computer screen, you may be less aware of copyright issues. Just because an artist has had a great idea doesn't mean you can copy it. What would you learn from copying? Just because you can, doesn't mean you have to. Interpretation is the key, and whether you are a tutor or a student, it is important to give credit to ideas that have inspired you which were first developed by someone else.

One issue that comes up in the world of exhibiting, whether it is at a craft show or a gallery, is the taking of photographs without permission. This is becoming a big issue. Cameras on mobile phones are wonderful for recording your own work and the inspiration you see around you, but visitors to shows and galleries seem to think nothing of happily clicking away, taking many photographs of an artist's work, never asking permission and feeling very hard done by when they are asked to stop. It is all about education. The better people understand the issues and the law, the better (hopefully) they will behave. It needs to start at school level, with teachers explaining this issue in the classroom. Unless there is a sign up saying you may take photographs, *always* ask permission before you do so. This applies particularly if you intend to publish the photographs on a social network site or your blog. You will be infringing copyright and intellectual property laws if you don't.

Finally

There has never been a more exciting time to be working in textiles. With people of so many different ages, nationalities and levels of experience practising at the same time, wonderful things are happening. We never stop learning. Do some research – try putting 'recycled clothes' in your search engine, and you will be amazed at the amount of information on just that subject. The popular social networks are also a great way to find others who are experimenting with unwanted materials. Whether you are a jeweller, a dressmaker, a textile artist or enjoy one of the many other visual arts, there will be something for you to try out. Rethinking the ways that you use materials in your work can be a challenge, but one thing is for sure: your work is unlikely to look like anyone else's. Innovate, don't imitate. Have fun, safely!

RIGHT Carrier-bag lace made by Judith Hammond (see page 79).

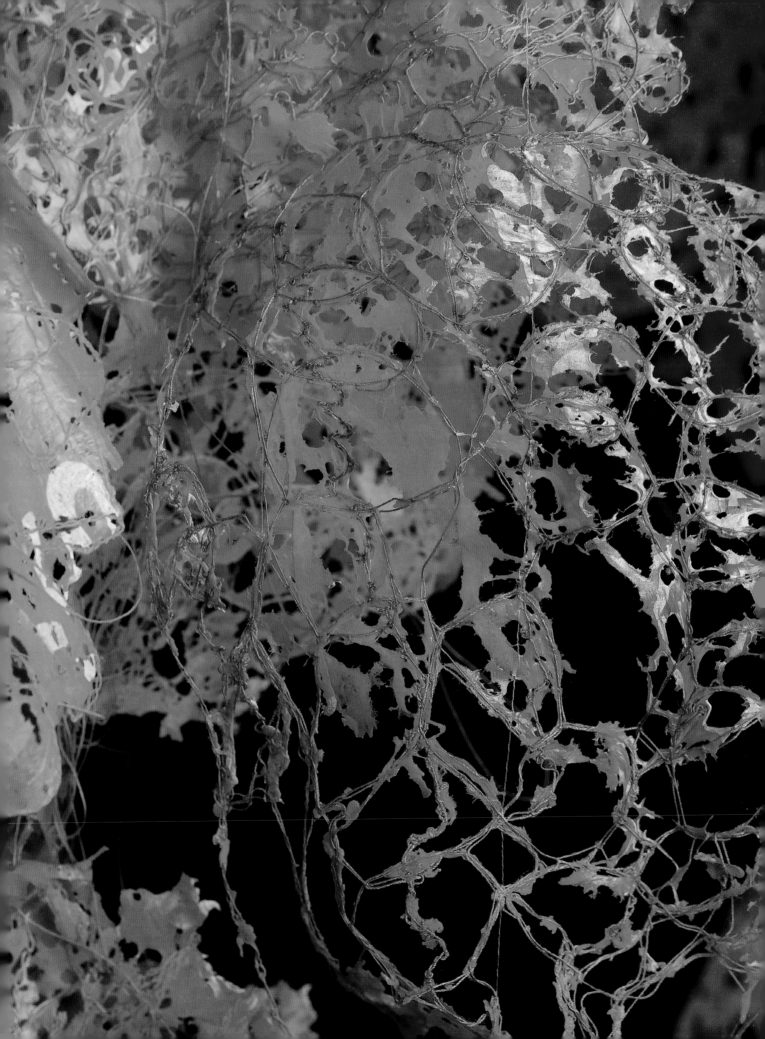

Featured artists

Angie Hughes
www.angiehughes.com

Anne Kelly
www.annekellytextiles.com

Cas Holmes
www.casholmes.textilearts.net

Claire Muir
www.clairemuir.co.uk

Helen McKenna
helenmckennasews.co.uk

Isobel Moore
www.isobelmoore.co.uk

Shaun West
info@kimthittichai.com

Janet Bolton
www.janetbolton.com

Jane Messent
info@kimthittichai.com

Jayne Routley
www.ladylazarus.co.uk

Judith Hammond
judith.hammond14@btinternet.com

Judy Martin
www.judymartin.co.uk

Kim Thittichai
www.kimthittichai.com

Laura Manning
lemanning@gmail.com

Mary Gray
mary.gray@btinternet.com

Mary Moox
marymoox@hotmail.com

Michelle Edinburgh
artcures@hotmail.co.uk

Ptolemy Elrington
www.hubcapcreatures.com

Sarah Hawkins
sarahjayhawkins@hotmail.co.uk

Sarah Patterson
Sarah.patterson@portsmouth-college.co.uk

Sissy Rooney
www.streetstylesurgery.co.uk

Stephanie Redfern
www.stephanieredfern.wordpress.com

Sue Culligan
www.knittingholidaysinfrance.com

Val Griffiths Jones
www.valgjones.com

Veronica Wells
info@kimthittichai.com

RIGHT Mary Moox's work
from page 106.

Useful addresses

nid-noi.com – mail order
S133, Solufleece, Solufix, Fuse n Tear, Hot Spots,
Lamifix, Stitch n Tear, Decovil 1 and Decovil 1 light,
Jones Tones transfer foils.
www.nid-noi.com

Art Van Go – mail order, shop and workshops
Fabulous paint selection, Acrylic wax, gilding flake,
mica flakes, Decovil 1 and Decovil 1 light, S133,
Procion dye and everything you could possibly desire.
The Studios, 1 Stevenage Road, Knebworth,
Hertfordshire SG3 6AN
art@artvango.co.uk
tel: +44 (0)1438 814946
fax: +44 (0)1438 81626
www.artvango.co.uk

**Colouricious – mail order, workshops and
craft holidays**
An amazing selection of wooden printing blocks
www.colouricious.com

Craftynotions.com – Mail order and shop
Colourful thoughts multi media paints, gilding flake,
dot jewels, mica flakes.
Craftynotions Ltd. Unit 2 Jessop Way, Newark
NG24 2ER
sales@craftynotions.com
tel+44 (0)1636 700862
fax +44 (0)1636 700862
www.craftynotions.com

Sissix – mail order
Die-cutting machines
www.sizzix.co.uk

Whaleys – mail order
The most comprehensive selection of fabrics for all
stitch, craft, dyeing, devore and so much more.
www.whaleys-bradford.ltd.uk

RIGHT *The Basingtstoke
Domesday Book* by Jane
Messant (see page 20).

RIGHT Brooches by Kim Thittichai (see page 72).

Bits and blogs

Kim Thittichai's blog
www.hot-textiles.blogspot.co.uk

Judy Martin's blog
www.judymartinpainter.wordpress.com

Cas Holmes' blogs
www.casholmes.blogspot.co.uk
www.magpieofthemind.blogspot.co.uk

Angie Hughes blog
www.angiestextilenotes.blogspot.co.uk

An excellent source of online workshops.
www.workshopontheweb.com

Maggie Grey's Blog
www.magstitch.blogspot.co.uk

A useful website with videos on how to use
Vilene products.
www.vilene-retail.com

Workshops and courses

Experimental Textiles with Kim Thittichai
www.experimentaltextiles.co.uk

Bobby Britnell runs her own excellent workshops and
also team teaches with Ruth Issett.
www.bobbybritnell.co.uk

Jamie Malden of Colouricious – block printing
workshops and textile trips to India
www.colouricious.com

Inkberrow Design Centre – workshops and
online courses
inkberrowdesigncentre.co.uk

Textile holidays in Spain
castanea-craft-courses.com

Creative workshops for young people
www.streetstylesurgery.co.uk

Online courses

Stitchbusiness – also has a fab newsletter
www.stitchbusiness.com

Dionne Swift
www.workshops-online.org

Distant Stitch
www.distantstitch.co.uk

Many of the artists featured in this book can also be
found on Facebook.

Further reading

Experimental Textiles
Kim Thittichai (Batsford)

Hot Textiles
Kim Thittichai (Batsford)

Layered Textiles
Kim Thittichai (Batsford)

Connected Cloth
Cas Holmes and Anne Kelly (Batsford)

The Found Object in Textile Art
Cas Holmes (Batsford)

Paper, Metal and Stitch
Maggie Grey and Jane Wild (Batsford)

Stitch and Structure
Jean Draper (Batsford)

Creative Recycling in Embroidery
Val Holmes (Batsford)

RIGHT Leaf sample
by Veronica Wells
(see page 55).

Index

A
Acrylic wax 13, 54, 60, 61, 70, 108, 111–112, 117
Anna Lee Wood 22
Angie Hughes 24,
Anne Kelly 98–101,
Appliqué 41, 99

B
Baking parchment 11, 13, 51, 53, 54, 59, 61, 70, 72, 78, 90, 108, 111, 115–117
Beads 75, 94, 110,
Bondaweb 10, 11, 51, 54, 70, 111–117,

C
Cas Holmes 98–101
Claire Muir 75, 90, 91
Copyright 118

D
Deco wadding 38,
Decovil 1 and Decovil 1 light 58, 67, 70, 108 & 109
Die-cutting machine 58, 60, 61, 72, 109
Dot jewels 11

E
Embossing powder 57
Embroidery 9, 20, 24, 27, 28, 35, 55, 73, 75, 78 –83, 87, 92, 94
Envelopes 44, 47

F
Faux chenille 56, 58, 59
Foil glue 13, 54
Fuse n Tear 48

G
Gel mediums 13, 105
Gilding flakes 58, 111

H
Heat gun/tool 78
Heat press 78
Heat transfer foil 54, 58, 112
Helen McKenna 30, 31
Hot Spots 7, 112, 115

I
Iron-on interfacing 25, 58, 59, 60, 67, 108
Isobel Moore 64, 94 & 95

J
Janet Bolton 17,
Jan Messant 20,
Jayne Routely 40,
Jones Tones transfer foils 10, 11, 54, 112, 115

Judith Hammond 7–83
Judy Martin 106 & 107

K
Kim Thittichai 56, 104, 105

L
Lamifix 109
Laura Manning 88–91

M
Mary Gray 84–87
Mary Moox 106
Mica flakes 11
Micro beads 57
Michelle Edinburgh 36

N
Newspaper 7, 50, 51, 53, 54, 55 –61, 65–70, 108, 112 –117

O
Owls 39

P
Paper 8, 20, 44, 48, 50, 60, 64, 70, 94, 98, 102, 105, 111, 112, 115
Paint 8,10, 21, 44, 48, 54, 55, 64, 67, 98, 102, 108
Photographs 48
Plastics 12, 67, 78, 84, 87–91
Polyester organza 58, 59
Printing blocks 48, 67, 112, 115
Procion dye 111
Ptomely Elrington 15

Q
Quilters Grid 32
Quickscreen Square 32
Quicksreen Triangle 32

S
S133 58, 60, 61, 72
Sarah Hawkins 47
Sarah Patterson 22
Shaun West 65–69,
Sew-in interfacing 58
Sissy Rooney 38
Sock monkey 36
Sock pigs 38
Soldering iron 78
Solufleece 8, 9, 55
Solufix 73
Stephanie Redfern 102 & 103
Stitch 9, 17, 24, 27, 28, 31, 32, 35, 38, 41, 44, 48, 50, 55, 70, 73, 84, 92, 94 & 95, 98, 102, 118
Stitch n Tear 112, 115
Sue Culligan 41

V
Val Griffith Jones 26
Veronica Wells 55

W
Water soluble 8
Wire 92, 95, 110

X
Xpandaprint 13

Glossary

Acrylic wax Acrylic medium with soft wax lustre finish. Used as a varnish.

Appliqué To decorate by cutting pieces of one material and applying it to the surface of another

Baking parchment A non stick paper used to protect your iron when using Bondaweb.

Bondaweb A web of glue on a backing paper. Used for appliqué and can also be painted.

Canvas Artist's canvas stretched over a wooden frame.

Couching Yarn or other materials are laid across the surface of the ground fabric and fastened in place with small stitches of the same or a different yarn.

Decovil 1 & Decovil 1 light Iron-on interfacing that feels like leather.

Die-cutting machine Die-cutting is like using a cookie cutter. A hand-operated, die-cutting machine uses steel rule die shapes to cut through a wide range of materials quickly and easily.

Embossing powders Embossing powder is a fast melting powder compound that can be applied to a smooth surface to create a raised image or configuration through the application of a mild source of heat.

Faux chenille Created by layering several fabrics, sewing channels in straight, concentric or curved lines and then cutting between the seams leaving the lowermost layer uncut.

Fencing wire A heavy gauge wire that keeps it shape when bent or shaped.

Fuse n tear A stabiliser for stitching onto stretch fabrics that can also be used to back fabric to enable the fabric to be printed through an inkjet printer.

Gel medium A variety of acrylic based finishes that dry clear and can be used as a glue or a varnish.

Gilding flake Fine flakes if metal – imitation gold leaf. Can be applied to Bondaweb and other glues.

Heat gun A heat tool used to distress synthetic fabric and melt embossing powders.

Heat press A machine engineered to imprint a design or graphic on a substrate, such as a t-shirt with the application of heat and pressure for a preset period of time. While heat presses are often used to apply designs to fabrics, they can also be used to imprint designs on mugs, plates, jigsaw puzzles, and other products.

Heat transfer foils Transfer foils add a metallic, holographic or other pattern to a surface by transferring a coating on the foil to the surface. Some type of adhesive is used to attract and hold the coating to the new surface. Use with Bondaweb or foil glue.

Herringbone stitch A traditional hand embroidery stitch.

Hot Spots Small spots of clear glue on a firm backing paper. Can be cut with scissors, hole punches or die cutting machines. The glue is transferred with heat and can be decorated with heat transfer foils.

Interfacing/interlining An iron-on or sew-in product made to support pattern pieces when making a garment or craft project.

Lamifix An iron-on plastic sheet sold by the metre that can make fabric waterproof.

Mica flakes Fine flakes of mica used to sprinkle onto painted Bondaweb or onto suitable glue.

Micro beads Very fine beads (without holes); can be sprinkled onto glues or into hot embossing powder.

Pigment/ochres All unearthed paints are tinted with earth and mineral pigments. These pigments give our paint a depth and radiance that cannot be mimicked by the chemical colorants used in conventional paints.

Polyester organza A fine synthetic fabric available in many colours that can be distressed with a heat gun and cut with a soldering iron.

Procion dye Fibre-reactive dyes for natural fabrics. In powder form. Particularly effective on cellulose based fibres (eg cotton, linen, viscose); they may be lighter and less predictable on wool and silk. Bright, clean, permanent colours. Colours are intermixable, or one colour can be dyed over another.

S133 The strongest iron-on interfacing available. Excellent for making three dimensional projects.

Scalpel A very sharp cutting tool used by surgeons that has been adopted by crafters.

Soldering iron A tool with a fine tip that is used in engineering. Lower wattage versions are used by crafters to distress and cut fabrics.

Solufix A self adhesive water soluble stabiliser.

Solufleece A water soluble stabiliser.

Stitch n tear A tear away stabiliser.

Synthetic A man-made fabric – eg. acrylic, nylon or acetate.

BELOW Brooches crafted from leftover 'pretties'.